I have known Antoinne for many years and have watched him mature. He has put his thoughts on paper to make life's journey easier for you. He has done a wonderful job.

Albert B. Ratner

Copyright © 2017 by Antoinne M. McKinney

All rights reserved. This book or any portion thereof may not be reproduced or used in any manner whatsoever without the express written permission of the publisher except for the use of brief quotations in a book review.

ISBN: 978-0-692-88073-9 (Paperback Edition)

Scriptures taken from the New King James Version®. Copyright © 1982 by Thomas Nelson. Used by permission. All rights reserved.

Printed in the United States of America

First Edition, 2017

Antoinne M. McKinney
PO Box 21394
Cleveland, OH 44121

www.AntoinneMMcKinney.com

THE INSPIRATION THAT LIES WITHIN...

Success Management & Planning

Antoinne M. McKinney

Contents

Preface..11
Success Management & Planning...................15
Understanding Success & Prosperity..............19
    The Instinct to Overcome............................20
    Success, what is it… really?.......................27
    Social Interference......................................30
    Social Influence...31
    How to Reach Success...............................34
Plan Your Goal the S.M.A.R.T. Way.................41
    S.M.A.R.T. Goal Planning...........................43
    Type of Goals..45
    The Planning Process.................................48
    Plan Execution..50
The Success Platform..55
    BUILD A FOUNDATION..............................57
    ALL YOU NEED IS THREE.........................57
    DEVELOP A CULTURE 58
Social & Professional Imagery..........................63
    Expressive...68

- Physical..70
- Qualities...73
- Image Types..74
- Use and Function....................................77
- Build Up Your Resume...................................79
  - Resume Fundamentals..............................85
  - How to Use a Resume...............................87
  - Improve Employment Opportunities............88
- It's All About Growth....................................91
  - Growth & Development Opportunities.......93
  - Identifying Assets....................................94
  - Evaluate All Aspects of Self......................97
  - Stretch Yourself......................................99
- Understanding Your Connectivity..................103
  - Networking & Social Groups....................115
  - Support Pyramid...................................118
  - The Layers of the Support Pyramid..........120
  - Making the Connection..........................125
- Financial Stewardship................................129
  - Value What You Have............................130

The Double-Edge Sword 133
Financial Responsibility 135
Steps for Financial Management 137
Message to the Reader 145
A Special Dedication 149
Acknowledgments 153
About the Author 157
What's Next 161
Write Down Your Dreams 162
Develop Your Strategic Approach 163
Assess How You rePresent Yourself 164
What Does This Mean For My Role? 165
SMART Goal Planning 167
SMART Goal Planning 168
Specify 168
Measure 169
Access 169
Rely 170
Time Frame 170
Self-Assessment 171

Success Management & Planning Self-Assessment...172

Type of Assessment...................................172

Academic Environment 172

Social Environment 173

Domestic Environment 173

Professional Environment 174

Preface

One day, early in the year of 2014, I found myself sitting at my desk in my cubicle area trying to figure out my next move in my professional career. I had thought to myself, "I spent nearly two years working long hours and I am barely making ends meet." I also knew that this would not be my situation for too long. One of my cubicle neighbors had started to make a major change in her life, which had been to relocate to another city. She had felt stagnate and the need to be in a new environment. Somehow, she believed that for her to have a successful career, she would have to leave Cleveland, Ohio. Quite often, she would ask me for some advice about her plans and her reasons for considering those ideas. In her opinion, she believed that I appeared to have a successful life, being that I am married, pursuing entrepreneurial ventures, and have a sense of direction for my future. One evening, while waiting for my wife to pick me up from work, I asked myself, "what helped me to get to where I am today?" At this point, I honestly did not know for sure if I had what it takes to really live a successful lifestyle. So, in the moment, I thought back to when I finally graduated from college in 2012, realizing that finishing college was a major obstacle for me to have overcome. Then, I began to examine how I managed to overcome the challenge to graduate from college as well as endure personal and social distractions in high school.

Altogether, including the two years I had been enrolled in the Post-Secondary Enrollment Options Program (PSEOP) at Cleveland State University, I invested a total of seven years pursuing an undergraduate college degree. I remembered that during high school and college, I struggled with balancing my personal, academic, and social aspects of life. Consequently, within the last five years of college, I received failing or below average grades for three consecutive years (2007-2010); had been placed on academic probation at three schools; transferred between schools twice; and dropped out of a community college to eventually earn a Bachelor's Degree in Urban Studies from Cleveland State University. As I reminisced on these moments, I realized that there must have been something inside of me that kept me from giving up. Could it have been the last words that I cherish from my great-great grandmother, "Make Me Proud." ...Or the fear of being a disappointment and embarrassment to my family? ...Or the car accident that took the life of my dear cousin at the age of twenty-five?

After I reflected on significant events in my life and the outcomes of my decisions, I recognized that there were several moments that ignited a spark of motivation, reminding me that I have a purpose for living. Despite those moments, I have identified several areas that I continuously work on to make sure that I am always in position for opportunities. In addition, not only has it been important for me to be ready when an opportunity presents itself, but also, I must learn how to maintain the energy, the drive, and the capacity to focus on excelling beyond my achievements, especially when there is no one around for support.

Let this book become a blessing to you as you discover principles, methodologies, and other inspirational concepts that have helped me become successful. I wrote this book seeing that my circumstances and situations were not so different than most people. Often my family and friends would find hope in me and become inspired to pursue dreams and goals. So, I hope that you, too, will discover the inspiration that lies within yourself to overcome obstacles and knock down the barriers that are blocking the pathway to your destiny.

Introduction
SUCCESS MANAGEMENT & PLANNING

Success Management & Planning is a lifestyle management curriculum that helps to develop a foundation for any person to achieve goals and reach various levels of success throughout their lifetime. This platform that you will learn to build will be sustained by five elements that contribute to your personal, educational, and professional growth, along with a lifetime experience of success. Before going into detail about the elements of this platform, it is essential to emphasize the difference that exist between success and prosperity. Their differences will help you to understand that the material possessions you receive, because of your successes, are merely gifts earned for your accomplishments. These rewards are disposable and do not define who you are nor measure the degree to which you can become successful.

Once you understand the basic principles of success and prosperity, you will then be ready to establish your success platform. The success platform is the foundation that consist of the five core elements, which you will build upon for the rest of your life. The five elements that have been identified to support the success platform are:

1. Social & Professional Imagery
2. Resume Building Techniques
3. Personal Assets (Resources & Skill)
4. Network & Support Groups
5. Financial Stewardship

These are essential areas that you will continue to nurture and develop, so that you can strategically position yourself to reach any level of success, in which you hope to achieve.

In the process of developing a plan to achieve your goal(s), you must identify the areas that will provide the most support for your strategic approach. These areas are like pillars that are used to stabilize a structure of a significant height. By understanding some basic principles in physics, I know that any structure can stand strong and firm on at least three legs or columns if they are positioned properly to stabilize that structure against opposing forces. For this reason, we will treat the elements in a similar manner to prepare you to become successful. By having at least three out of the five elements involved in the planning process, you will be in a good and secure position to achieve any of your personal, professional, or academic aspirations.

Once you have learned how these five elements can support your goals, use them to assess yourself and how you live. These elements are also areas that can impact your personal growth by strengthening your character, improving your self-esteem, building your confidence, and creating a sense of enthusiasm for life and your future. You should always aspire for greatness and aim to achieve beyond your last accomplishment. Grow to become prosperous with skills and knowledge, but live in prosperity by developing a healthy lifestyle and becoming valuable to others.

Chapter One
UNDERSTANDING SUCCESS & PROSPERITY

Life is full of experiences. Experiences that will bring joy to your spirit... or those that cause emotional heartache. All our experiences help us to develop and shape who we are. I wonder if you have heard this phrase spoken before, "you win some and you will lose some." This subtle statement tells us that in life we will encounter difficulties, successes and failures, rights and wrongs, and many other instances where the chance to experience the good and the bad are inevitable. Although this may be true for all people, I feel that we acknowledge the results of our experiences more than we take the time to truly honor the process that gets us to the place we end up. It appears the only time we tend to address the process of anything that we do is when we receive a result that we did not expect or when we decide to help someone else get positive results in their life.

A result is the outcome after decisions have been made and actions have been executed. For instance, a graduation is the result of someone deciding to commit to a specific learning experience and putting forth the required amount of effort to excel, at least, per the minimum standards. So, the result of your experience is determined by a decision and the actions that follow. Therefore, since life is full of experiences, your life will become the result of many decisions and the actions that accompany those decisions. So, from the moment you are conceived, the choices and actions of your parents are molding your life. Then, soon after you are born, your future will become what you desire and strive after.

The Instinct to Overcome

During the infancy stage and throughout our childhood, we all, at some point, acted in a manner to gain attention from others and most often probably an adult. By the nature of being a child, we continue to display behaviors that attract attention toward us. Because of our actions, we will eventually receive attention, but not always, the attention that we had hoped to receive, which may have been a simple response of delight and encouragement. Children ultimately look for attention because they are looking to develop a relationship with the persons that constantly appear in their life. From birth, a child naturally desires and yearns for comfort from their mother and over time the father will experience moments of his son or daughter wanting him, if he is *present*. During the nine months in the womb, the baby has developed a unique connection with his or her mother that eventually creates a dependency for survival. Once born and separated by the severing of the umbilical cord, the baby then becomes dependent on the mother for feeding and comfort. The behaviors of an infant draws attention, but only for the satisfaction of their biological needs and the feeling of security. Once the relationship between the child and parent(s) have been established, they begin to learn how to understand one another, which takes time.

Principles for Raising a Child

"Even a child is known by his deeds, whether what he does is pure and right. **Therefore,** *train up a child in the way he should go, and when he is old he will not depart from it.* **By the nature of humanity,** *foolishness is bound up in the heart of a child; the rod of correction will drive it far from him. Do not withhold correction from a child, for if you* **chasten** *him with a rod, he will not die. The father of the righteous will greatly rejoice; and he who begets a wise child will delight in him.* **Please be reminded that** *the rod and rebuke give wisdom, but a child left to himself brings shame to his mother."*

This message was inspired by the following biblical scriptures, Proverbs 20:11; 22:6, 15; 23:13, 24; and 29:15, respectively.

The Inspiration That Lies Within...

I compiled this message from a series of scriptures out of the book of Proverbs to encourage people who are raising children to remain active in their child's growth. As parents and adults that oversee children, we have an important role that will influence the direction of a child's life. From the time of their birth, both parents and their child(ren), will endure a journey discovering and learning each other. Developing communication will be an important phase of the parent-child relationship. Babies that weep, whine, and squeal are often expressing themselves. When there is somewhat a baseline for parents to understand their child and vice versa, the child presumably knows how to gain attention. Some parents can catch on to the communicative cues quicker than others, but nonetheless, become more aware of such behaviors and learn what the child is expressing. The reason is that you want to make sure over time your son or daughter does not craft manipulation because it can become a part of their ongoing behavior. In addition, children adopt behaviors from what they observe and from what they can do, so take heed to these principles and apply them. You will see that with your constant enforcement, your children will grow up with a healthy outlook on life.

Although the parent-child relationship is important for the child's development, there are other people that will interact with him or her throughout their time of growth. You have relatives, neighbors, teachers, daycare providers, and many other individuals that have different roles and they will engage with your child(ren) accordingly. Children that get exposure to other people, especially those with a significant role in their upbringing, become curious and encouraged to become observant of people and their surroundings. As children become more observant, they will try to mimic behaviors and discover new objects as they see them. In my opinion, this is the best example of socialization. Before children de-

velop clear speech they are learning how to adapt to a new world, while gaining a sense of independence from the nine months of dependency in the womb.

So, after years of exploration, discovery, and development, your baby boy or girl grew into a toddler, then became a preschooler, and now is entering their years of grade school. So, over the past five or six years, your child should have succeeded many milestones since they were born. The continued succession of these milestones came from the constant desire to try to do what they have seen. Of course, there was a biological process to it all, but it was still a *process*. It took time, patience, support, resources, and other factors for children to triumph these milestones over a period. It is a part of our human nature to grow, which means that we have what it takes to succeed over obstacles as they come before us.

By this time, as your son or daughter enters grade school they have become exposed to many challenges and within their own time they have found a way to overcome the challenges with constant effort. Grade school brings about different challenges that can become overwhelming to a child because from this point forward, time is an essential factor to a child's development. Children at the grade school age will be learning social, mental, physical, and life skills, in addition to, gaining more awareness of their capacity in these areas. With a little help and guidance, the children will reach satisfactory or beyond so they can move on to new expeditions in this journey of life. One day someone will eventually ask your child this question, "What do you want to be when you get older?" What should your child say? How does a child even know what they would like to be when they grow up? How did YOU process this question when YOU were a child?

Depending on the era that you were raised in, the things you were exposed to may have influenced your response. For example, the roles of an adult as you were exposed to them, the characters you have once watched on television... or have read in the comic or story books... or even from the folktales that have been passed down from generations to give moral lessons about life. From these various stories, you probably remember what sparked your attention and motivated you to begin thinking about life beyond your childhood.

When I was a child, I aspired to be like the superheroes that I watched on television - Batman, Superman, Mega Man, Sonic the Hedgehog, the red Power Ranger, and several others. When I aspired to be like these characters, it was not because I wanted to do what they did, but I was encouraged to have the kind of character they portrayed as I watched them fight for good and the well-being of others. Most of the bad characters or villains always sought fame, prestige, or monetary wealth, but never prevailed, so I learned early that the benefit of living is not about the richness of materialism, but rather the wealth of good character.

> Principle #1: Character is Worth More Than Material Richness
>
> *"A good name is to be chosen rather than great riches,*
> *Loving favor rather than silver and gold."*
> *(Proverbs 22:1 NKJV)*
>
> I had been living by this principle before I even learned about it. Growing up, I always associated good behavior with rewards. My family raised me with the understanding that if my performance and behavior was great I could almost receive anything that I had asked for. This started primarily when I began grade school and continued to become a habit, even still unto this day. When I read this scripture as a teenager, I began to understand more of the divine implication of this behavior. I realized wealth is not obtained through vast amounts of money, but rather earned through the character of a person.

If you do not know me well, it can be easy for you to assume that I have been fortunate because of the resources I have. But, what you do not know is that because I applied this principle in my life and made it a solid part of my character, I have been given a degree of favor that has given me the provision to receive access to resources and exposure to opportunities. I say this to you because you will not know what is promised to you unless you act within the reasonable expectations required of you, so that you may gain your rewards.

Do you know what sparked your aspirations as a child? It is important to understand or recognize what inspires your aspirations. Knowing the source of your goals lets you know what fuels your desire to succeed. Success is an occurrence that can be experienced at different levels, but it always starts with a vision. After doing some research on how success is experienced, I discovered seven ways that describe how you may experience success:

1. **A Vision Realized - Watch your faith manifest itself into existence.** *(Now faith is the substance of things hoped for, the evidence of things not seen. For by it the elders obtained a good testimony. By faith we understand that the worlds were framed by the word of God, so that the things which are seen were not made of things which are visible. Hebrews 11:1-3 NKJV)*

2. **The Product of Obedience - The fulfillment of someone's request of your ability.** *(Now therefore, if you will indeed obey My voice and keep My covenant, then you shall be a special treasure to Me above all people; for all the earth is Mine. Exodus 19:5 NKJV)*

3. **Accountability - Being responsible for your own actions or the lack thereof.** *(And why do you look at the speck in your brother's eye, but do not consider the plank in your own eye? Or how can you say to your brother, 'Let me remove the speck from*

your eye'; and look, a plank is in your own eye? Hypocrite! First remove the plank from your own eye, and then you will see clearly to remove the speck from your brother's eye. Matthew 7:3-5 NKJV)

4. **Acceptance with Understanding - Being content in the moment, knowing the reason you received results or experienced events in the manner that they occurred.** *(Trust in the Lord with all your heart, And lean not on your own understanding; In all your ways acknowledge Him, And He shall direct your paths. Proverbs 3:5-6 NKJV)*

5. **Adaptability - The ability to adjust when circumstances change.** *(My brethren, count it all joy when you fall into various trials, knowing that the testing of your faith produces patience. But let patience have its perfect work, that you may be perfect and complete, lacking nothing. If any of you lacks wisdom, let him ask of God, who gives to all liberally and without reproach, and it will be given to him. James 1:2-5 NKJV)*

6. **Sacrifice - Living for the sake of others more than yourself.** *(I beseech you therefore, brethren, by the mercies of God, that you present your bodies a living sacrifice, holy, acceptable to God, which is your reasonable service. And do not be conformed to this world, but be transformed by the renewing of your mind, that you may prove what is that good and acceptable and perfect will of God. For I say, through the grace given to me, to everyone who is among you, not to think of himself more highly than he ought to think, but to think soberly, as God has dealt to each one a measure of faith. Romans 12:1-3 NKJV)*

7. **Commitment - Dedicating your life for a greater purpose with discipline and faith.** *(Commit your works to the Lord, And your thoughts will be established. Proverbs 16:3 NKJV; If a man makes a vow to the Lord, or swears an oath to bind himself by some agreement, he shall not break his word; he shall do according to all that proceeds out of his mouth. Numbers 30:2 NKJV; And whatever you do, do it heartily, as to the Lord and not*

to men, knowing that from the Lord you will receive the reward of the inheritance; for you serve the Lord Christ. Colossians 3:23-24 NKJV)

Can you recall experiencing success at any of the levels listed? If so, take a moment to describe, at least, one instance for each level that you believe you have experienced. After writing down these events, what have you noticed? Did each of the events you described require the same amount of effort? Did you do the same things to achieve what you had accomplished? You may have recognized that each experience was different and required a variety of actions from your efforts.

Society recognizes successful people by their image portrayed in public or by the value of their material possessions that they may have or can afford. Every individual has their own personal meaning of success, which makes it hard for someone growing up to decide what to pursue in life. What I want to help you understand is that success is more than an option and an experience, it is a lifestyle executed every day.

Success, what is it... really?

It is common for people to associate success with a lifestyle that appears to be less problematic and filled with material possessions because of that individual's financial position or freedom. More often, people at some point in life become attracted to the presentation of "successful people" by what the media displays through entertainment and the news. From this point of view, you can probably imagine how you defined success based on what you've observed. The pure nature of success is much more than what you can see or feel, but rather experience in a lifetime.

If you grew up with the hope to become successful by reaching the image of or becoming a certain kind of person, you probably were encouraged by what you have seen on television, or read in a book, or viewed in a magazine. According to the dictionary, the definition of success is the achievement of something planned or attempted; in addition, it is something that turns out or results as you may have planned or intended. By this definition, it is safe to assume that success is that moment experienced when a goal, task, or standard has been met. Therefore, becoming successful by this concept seems like it can be more attainable rather than trying to live up to an image.

Just as the media misrepresents the image of success, prosperity can easily become misunderstood by the image that is most often portrayed through media as well. When the media associates a certain image to prosperity it typically shows an excessive amount of valuable possessions owned by a person, family, group, or company. These valuable items can be determined by their quality, rareness, cost, historic importance, and many other unique characteristics. But, these kinds of things are generally collected by those individuals that not only can afford them, but also respects them. On the other hand, the image of prosperity can be displayed in the media with the intention to persuade others to believe that a certain kind of person who is prosperous does certain things, goes to certain places, acts a certain way, and acquires certain kinds of behaviors and habits. The false reality to these things, although there is little truth to them, is that prosperity is having an abundance of valuable possessions and living a lifestyle to receive these things.

Prosperity is a successful, flourishing, or thriving condition, especially in financial respects; good fortune. In the dictionary, prosperity is correlated to excessive financial gain, but we are going to go beyond the finances and redefine prosperity in a more obtainable manner. So, let's redefine prosperity as a successful, flourishing, or thriving condition, and a lifestyle that resembles growth and sustainability. This may sound like a lot to understand right now, but I will break it down for you. In this definition, there are several elements that create the condition of prosperity; but keep in mind that these elements are like ingredients, they are necessary and must be present for prosperity to exist. First, in the new definition, we know that it includes being *successful*, which means that at an average rate you are more than likely to achieve goals and meet the standards that are required of you. The second element of prosperity is your potential or ability to *flourish*, in other word, your work effort reflects that you strive for excellence in the things that you do. Now the third element in prosperity refers to the condition of *thriving*, which is a circumstance that presents itself to be healthy and supports continued growth. Thriving also represents an ongoing experience to simultaneously consist of growth, success, progression in the areas that you prosper. The fourth element about prosperity, which I believe is a very important concept, is that a person truly experiences prosperity when it becomes a part of their lifestyle. Therefore, when prosperity is experienced in your life it should be evident throughout your habits, your behavior, your attitude, and the principles you choose to live by. By doing so, you confirm that you aim to grow while you maintain stability in all areas of your life.

So, behind all the material possessions, the favor, the social status, and financial advantages, there are ethics and values that contribute to the reason prosperous people can do the things that they do and have the things that they have. Now you may ask yourself, "does your life reflect a path going into prosperity?' If not, there are possibly some areas in your life that can be improved upon or re-evaluated to get you closer to experience prosperity.

Hopefully, this has brought clarity to your understanding of success and prosperity. I want you to focus on the basics, in terms of the primary elements that make up success. It is very important that you develop a simple understanding of success and ignore the image that our society displays what success should look like. You will experience success at different levels and in separate areas of your life that will one day lead you into a lifestyle full of prosperity.

Since success is the "achievement of something," you can set a goal to be as simple as waking up in the morning, brushing your teeth, and eating breakfast before you head off to start your day. This may sound very easy written down, but if you have no experience or consistency doing either of these tasks, this goal can very well present many challenges making it difficult to achieve. For instance, if you are poor at managing your time, it will be difficult for you to assume that you will wake up on time. It may be best for you to prepare yourself for the next morning on the night before, so that you will not have so much to do before you leave home.

Success can teach us about the importance of preparation and planning for things we hope to manage. So, as you continue to adopt the new definitions that we established about success and prosperity, be aware that there are multiple ways to achieve success and reach prosperity.

Social Interference

As you travel on your journey to reach success, you will encounter obstacles, distractions, challenges, and even moments when you may feel like you need to change your course of direction or your entire approach. In the United States, our society is so diverse with nationalities, cultures, ethnicities, and opportunities that we are inclined to the influence of other people. Exposure to other people and their customs may have an influence on our thoughts, our behaviors, and our emotions. In addition, their customs can also encourage or disrupt how we perceive ourselves, the life we are living, and even the opportunities that approach us. These kind of influences can be associated with the concept of social interference. Social interference is any action, conflict or activity that may interrupt, hamper, or stop a person's activity. The main point to grasp from this concept is that your social exposure will have the potential to create change in your life that can yield more growth or reduce the chance to advance in your life.

Social Influence

Success is something that almost everyone in the world tries to reach. Our society often promotes success as a lifestyle that includes lavishness, wealth, blue or white collar careers, fame, and prestige. For instance, some television shows, movies, and celebrities portray this concept, while creating social trends that people attempt to adopt. This kind of influence can become a distraction to people, encouraging behaviors, attitudes, and habits that are meant to resemble successful lifestyles. Our young people are being tainted by these mixed messages that are often shared through various media outlets. This may contribute toward the reason young people tend to disregard their priorities such as being attentive to and engaged in their education. Nowadays young people seem to have more interest in pursuing promoted lifestyles from entertainers rather than learning what future opportunities are available to consider for their careers.

When a person gets caught up with social trends their priorities become altered and often begin to idolize the behaviors of celebrities, entertainers, or others that may grab their attention. Priorities are often affected because the individual's focus shifts from what is most important to what is more interesting or desired. For instance, it is common for teenagers and young adults to give up on their education and pursue employment because it becomes difficult for them to rationalize the value of how the information being taught in class directly relates to their life. With these standardized tests being issued to assess the education system, the teaching styles of our educators are becoming affected. Thus, the learning environment changes and teachers are influenced to emphasize their learning material based on the tests and less on the relevance to how skills and principles apply to their own life experiences. The social trends and the behaviors of people seen throughout the media are more attractive to young people. These individuals in mainstream media often share how their beginnings are closely related to what their audience may experience in their lives. Youth that are members of a low-income household, or live below the poverty line focus solely on survival and how to change their living conditions or circumstances.

Have you or anyone that you know compared your lives to that of another person's achievements, career path, financial status, and living condition? In other words, have you viewed the lifestyle of someone who is successful and made it the model for your own success? By doing this, you are adding pressure to yourself before you even know what your capacity is to achieve your own goals. *Social influence is characterized as the moment when others affect your emotions, opinions, or behaviors.* Therefore, suggesting you will become influenced by someone else's opinions or lifestyle habits. Since, social influence can be disguised in many different forms and experienced in so many ways, I have listed and briefly described a few types of social influence. Take your time to understand and realize how they may affect your decisions and the way you may pursue your opportunities in life.

Conformity. Conformity is the change in belief or behavior to fit in with a group; or follow standards, rules, or laws; or actions in accord with prevailing social standards, attitudes, practices, etc. What would cause someone to feel the need to conform to any norm in society…or neighborhood…or group? Research expresses that certain pressures brought on by groups or peers can influence people to conform to certain norms that are caused by bullying, persuasion, teasing, criticism, and other similar circumstances. The desire to conform can come from a person's desire to be liked, to be correct, or to affiliate oneself to a social role.

Socialization. Socialization is the process by which people learn from others to function in life. Growing up as a child you learn how to say words, how to walk and how to do many other things from observing others as they interact with and around you. Observing is a way to learn and pick up habits that can be either good or bad. The things that you observe and put into practice may eventually become habits that you adopt into your own lifestyle. These habits can also be a way in which you choose to accomplish things. The influence of socialization can also be adopted as a means of survival depending on your living conditions and circumstances.

Peer Pressure. Peer pressure is a type of social influence that is often associated with the encouragement of negative behavior and unhealthy decision making. Peer Pressure is an influence from members of one's peer group and can either be direct or indirect. Direct pressure normally results in being put on the spot and on the verge of being embarrassed or threatened. Indirect pressure comes from the influence of someone's actions, behaviors, or appearances that are captivating or considered the norm. It is easy for someone to feel pressured if they are being singled out or feeling different than everybody else. Having success in life highly depends on making positive decisions with a clear mind and conscious. If someone is persuasive in guiding you along the way, you still deserve the right to feel comfortable in the process to earn your rewards from what you aspire to achieve.

Persuasion. Persuasion is a type of social influence that uses someone's beliefs (morals, values, principles, etc.) to yield another person's thoughts, motives, attitude, and behaviors to a specific frame of mind. Persuasion is a technique that is often used to manipulate, encourage, or threaten someone so that they can act in support of a cause or an occurrence. This method of influence is meant to convey an individual to believe in something predicated on what that person already believes, understands, or even supports.

Sometimes you may find yourself in situations where you feel ignored, not loved, unappreciated, or even misunderstood. The need to feel liked, loved, or wanted is common for people including our youth, for this reason, they are more likely to conform to social norms. Changing your behaviors or beliefs to anything other than habits, morals, and values that are positive, may result into undesirable behaviors that can divert you away from the path that will lead you to your destiny in life.

How to Reach Success

There are many ways in which a person can reach success as well as measure their progression until they have obtained it. I want to help dismantle the *status quo* that society has implicated to determine if a person is successful. First, you need to learn how to set and pursue your goals. Most often, people set goals that require a significant amount of work to be accomplished. All the work that needs to be done should be measurable by tracking the progression toward a goal. If a goal seems too overwhelming, more than likely, people will get discouraged or hesitate in their attempt to pursue it. Creating goals that become daunting is such a bad practice and happens quite frequently. In order to avoid this habit, you will need to learn how to <u>organize your goals</u> and <u>recognize the different methods</u> to achieve them, while complimenting your willingness and abilities.

I realized, just about every day, I try to get *something* accomplished, regardless of how big or small the task may seem. By acting in this manner, I have developed a habit of achieving bigger goals, by breaking them down into smaller increments to accomplish. For instance, my daily goals are generally centered around the management and balancing of responsibilities that I have at home, at work or school, and other associations where I have a commitment. Some of my daily goals have developed into a normal routine, until the moment I have achieved the major goal I originally set out to accomplish. If you would like to adopt this method into your lifestyle, try adding a necessary or healthy habit that you can focus for no longer than 30 minutes.

Success is, not only achieved by setting goals and accomplishing them, but also mentally associating your routines with the concept of being successful. Secondly, you must understand that success needs to become an everyday practice in all aspects of your life. This means that you must develop a mindset that affiliates the completion of routines, tasks, and the fulfillment of your purpose to a degree of success. So yes, brushing your teeth, eating your meals, doing homework, showing up on time, and taking care of your household are all part of the process to become successful. When you allow success to be a part of your routine, eventually, you will develop a conscious or "sense of urgency" that will influence your desire to get things accomplished. By the nature of this new mindset, you will find yourself developing small things for yourself to do throughout the day. These small items on your to-do list will help you to feel the progression as you move closer to your more significant goal(s). Specifically, I have been able to identify seven ways to get things accomplished; and I also grouped them into four categories.

Standards. Standards can be described as a set of measures, rules, actions, or responsibilities that are given within the reasonable means of someone's ability. Standards are a good way to enforce discipline, accountability, and other qualities for individual growth. There are two types of standards that are great tools to use that will help you stay focused and committed – *tasks* and *expectations*. Tasks are a piece of work expected to be completed or undertaken. From this definition, I need you to understand that a task is a "portion" of total work that needs to be done, rather than the entire responsibility. For example, if you aim to clean your kitchen, you are not going to do everything all at once. You will, in different moments, focus on smaller tasks like sweeping the floor, washing the dishes, and cleaning the surfaces. Expectations are the anticipation of something within reason. Expectations are a measure that allows you or someone else to hold you accountable for your responsibilities. Expectations can be used to encourage growth by challenging a person to do a task, although he or she may not believe or know they can do it. This type of pressure can help to strengthen your faith and expand your belief in areas where you are challenged.

Hierarchy. Next, you can reach a level of success through a hierarchy, which is a system or classification for ranking levels, positions, or people within an organization, family, or group. When you advance through a hierarchy, you are placed in positions of respect, humility, and accountability. These positions, not only demand respect, humility, and accountability from others, but also reciprocate these qualities to those in lower ranks. One of the ways to experience the benefits of a hierarchy is through inheritance; this is the transfer of ownership by way of relationship or entitlement. You may be aware of this process because it is most often exercised when property or a person's possessions are passed on to someone of close relation. An inheritance is not given to someone because of the value that something may be worth, but rather to entrust that person will respect, honor and properly care for those valuables. An inheritance is commonly passed on to the next generation or heir(s) to carry on the responsibility and the expectations of a legacy. Heirs should be carefully chosen and possess certain qualities and characteristics to be prepared for the responsibility.

Succession, quite like an inheritance, is the coming of one person or thing in a sequential order. Succession and inheritance are closely related, except for the fact that succession follows an ordered system that causes an assumed shift, whereas, inheritance involves the judgment of a person's ability to handle tasks and certain responsibilities. Succession is also most commonly associated with roles of leadership and things that develop overtime, through a process.

Qualification. Another way for someone to reach success is by their qualifications, which are suitable characteristics or skills, for a purpose. One of the reasons for qualifications is to evaluate the competitive advantage a person may have during a competition. Competitions occur beyond sports and games, they are experienced in many aspects of our society. You compete for employment, education, relationships, attention by others, and the consumption of products and services. Competitions are good to measure a person's skill level and their areas of strength. In addition, competitions are an excellent way to identify specific areas for growth.

Qualifications also measure your competence, which is being adequate or sufficient in ability and skill, for a purpose. It is very important that you continue learning because your competence level can help you deal with different situations and position you to take advantage of opportunities. Your competence increases as you begin to practice skills and apply your knowledge through problem solving and critical thinking. The best time to practice your skills and apply what you know is when you have someone that can give you guidance and assess your strengths and weaknesses.

Qualifications will always have a significant role in how you reach your goals and obtain success in life. Practically, you will experience many occasions that will require you to compete for opportunities. Likewise, your competence in different areas will always have an impact on how well you perform tasks and manage responsibilities.

Planning. Last, but not least, the most significant way to achieve success is by *planning* it. As we all may come to recognize, things do not always turn out as we plan them; but the plan illustrates the process we must undergo to get where we need to be in life. The dictionary defines planning as the process of organizing thoughts and ideas in a way to make possible. The most common way for anyone to achieve success, in this manner, is through goal setting. Goal setting is how you would generally establish a plan to reach attainable short-term or long-term goals. Goal setting is unique because you will combine the use of the other ways we've listed to accomplish many action items that you might specify in your strategic plan. In the next chapter, you learn how to organize and plan the goals you wish to establish.

Success is not a "spur of the moment" phenomenon, it is a concept that involves preparation, planning, and some form of action to take place for it to occur. For instance, in order to be on time for an appointment or any other event, you do not just let things happen, you either schedule or plan to attend. Your timing or schedule of events may also lead you to be in position to accomplish things that were not on your plan to achieve. In most instances, I can say that every person has experienced success at some time or another in life. The issue that is burdensome to people is that success may not occur as often as they may desire to experience it. Therefore, something should change, more than likely it is your mindset or how you think about success. Before you can change your actions, you must change your mind, but even then, you still will need to alter your thought process as well.

Principle #2: Change Your Thinking, So the World Around You Will Be Different

"And do not be conformed to this world, but be transformed by the renewing of your mind, that you may prove what is that good and acceptable and perfect will of God." (Romans 12:2 NKJV)

One of the hardest things you can do in life is change your mind. As often as you may have heard it or will hear it in your lifetime, it takes a lot of effort to eventually think differently. Your thoughts and actions synchronize together and affect one another. The irony about this is that whatever you think about most, you will eventually do. Likewise, what you do often will trigger your thoughts to do it again. The best way to change your mind is to also change what you do or how you do it, so that the result will one day be different and more acceptable based on the standards you choose to live by.

"This I say, therefore, and testify in the Lord, that you should no longer walk as the rest of the Gentiles walk, in the futility of their mind, having their understanding darkened, being alienated from the life of God, because of the ignorance that is in them, because of the blindness of their heart; who, being past feeling, have given themselves over to lewdness, to work all uncleanness with greediness. But you have not so learned Christ, if indeed you have heard Him and have been taught by Him, as the truth is in Jesus: that you put off, concerning your former conduct, the old man which grows corrupt according to the deceitful lusts, and be renewed in the spirit of your mind, and that you put on the new man which was created according to God, in true righteousness and holiness.

Therefore, putting away lying, 'Let each one of you speak

truth with his neighbor,' for we are members of one another. 'Be angry, and do not sin': do not let the sun go down on your wrath, nor give place to the devil. Let him who stole steal no longer, but rather let him labor, working with his hands what is good, that he may have something to give him who has need. Let no corrupt word proceed out of your mouth, but what is good for necessary edification, that it may impart grace to the hearers. And do not grieve the Holy Spirit of God, by whom you were sealed for the day of redemption. Let all bitterness, wrath, anger, clamor, and evil speaking be put away from you, with all malice. And be kind to one another, tenderhearted, forgiving one another, even as God in Christ forgave you." (Ephesians 4:17-32 NKJV)

Chapter Two
PLAN YOUR GOAL THE S.M.A.R.T. WAY

With a new way to define success and a different understanding of how to gain prosperity, do you believe you are successful?

If you answered, **yes**, then ask yourself what do you need to do to experience a successful lifestyle?

If you believe otherwise and feel that you have not reached the level of success that you desire, figure out what you need to do to finally get there?

Regardless of where you believe you stand with the original question, your action or response will remain the same. In either scenario, you shall realize that you will need to develop a strategic plan that will guide you through a process to achieve your goals. As I stated at the end of chapter one, success does not result from the occurrence of random events nor is it a "spur of the moment" phenomenon. Neither does successful people believe that they, themselves, are so great that they can wake up each day deciding whether it is a favorable time for them to achieve a goal. What really happens is that every successful person creates a plan, one that provides ideas and reasonably outlines possible ways to reach his or her goal(s).

The secret to having a successful plan is that it should be **adjustable.** Adjustable, in such a way that it allows for you to have the flexibility to make changes wherever and whenever it may be necessary or as your circumstances may change. Sometimes when people strive to reach a goal, they experience unexpected events, especially those that are uncontrollable. Instead of allowing events that are out of your control to become a distraction, you must become focused enough to alter from your original plan and adjust to a different approach. For people to reach a level of success and live a prosperous life, they should learn how to adjust along the way and become accustomed to "change."

Principle #3: Plan the Process, Then Prepare to Receive

Planning is not anticipating the outcome, but rather preparing your outlook for where you hope to go. Planning creates a perspective approach for you to execute a series of actions that will lead you somewhere. Plans are uncertain, but they guarantee you a chance to have certainty. At least with a plan, you will have an idea of what is required to reach your destiny.

The process of planning is an act of diligence that allows an individual to consider factors involved that somehow affect you. Planning helps to evaluate conditions, circumstances, and the cost to pursue your goal. In addition, planning evaluates your ability, effort, and effectiveness.

For which of you, intending to build a tower, does not sit down first, and count the cost, whether he has enough to finish it — (Luke 14:28 NKJV)

He who has a slack hand becomes poor, but the hand of the diligent makes rich. (Proverbs 10:4 NKJV)

The plans of the diligent lead surely to plenty, but those of everyone who is hasty, [lead] surely to poverty. (Proverbs 21:5 NKJV)

S.M.A.R.T. Goal Planning

Since I believe you have a sincere interest to live successfully, I would like to introduce you to the *S.M.A.R.T. Goal Planning* process that I use to help prepare me for goals that I intend to pursue. Originally, the SMART concept for goal setting was developed by George T. Doran, who created this process to bring about results within different levels of management to make deliverables, in other words, create tasks that are attainable. This concept was not intended to become a checklist of variables to show progression toward achieving project and academic goals. Over the past years, this concept grew and has been modified for adoption by management teams, teachers, students, and others that are reaching for success.

The founding concept that Mr. Doran developed was good, but it became difficult for me to organize my thoughts to develop a strategic plan for the goals I wanted to achieve. The original five areas that Doran defined for SMART were specific, measurable, assignable, realistic, time related.

- **S**pecific – targets a specific area for improvement
- **M**easurable – quantify or suggest an indicator of progress
- **A**ssignable – specify who will do it
- **R**ealistic – states what results can be realistically achieved, given available resources.
- **T**ime related – specify when the results can be achieved

For professionals and projects, these areas or criteria are important for accomplishing complex goals that require a group of people. After a while, I thought about how I could overcome challenges and reach my goals while being a teenager and in the first five years of my twenties. Comparing the original SMART concept to the components that I realized are essential to the way I have reached my goals, I discovered similarities and two unique components that differ slightly from Dr. Doran's criteria. The areas essential to me were *accessible resources* and *reliability*. Before we go any further, I would like to make a distinction in Dr. Doran's concept. The five components in SMART are often considered *criteria*, which would imply that these components would be necessary to meet a certain standard. For the *S.M.A.R.T. Goal Planning* process, the five components are not measures to meet a standard, but rather components that are important for creating a plan. These components are designed so that the dynamics of goal setting can be simplified for any person to understand how to pursue a specific goal.

The *S.M.A.R.T. Goal Planning* process will be a tool for you to develop strategies for a plan to reach your goals. This process is useful for different types of goals including, but not limited to, educational, career exploration, job placement for entry level workers, employment for experienced workers, and financial management. Having goals are essential to your personal growth because goals, not only helps us to aim for hopes and dreams, but also challenges our character, skills, and other abilities. Everyone regardless of age or stage in life should consider learning how to create and use goals throughout their lifetime. From the time a baby starts to get curious, aspirations help the baby grow into a child and from a child to an adult.

Type of Goals

Educational Goals. Educational goals focus on the growth of an individual's learning ability. Parents typically encourage learning to their children when they help their babies learn to crawl, walk, eat, potty and do other developmental skills. The praises that children get for making their parents proud create a sense of inspiration that builds confidence and courage. This is an example of what is likely to occur once you have overcome a challenge, you become strengthened, both physically and mentally. Once children start school the transition of learning shifts primarily from physical to mental, but depending on how a child is raised, this could potentially bring about significant challenges for children to learn. With all the changes occurring throughout our nation's education system, it is becoming more difficult for children to value their primary and secondary educational experiences. We are living in a time when there is a significant emphasis on state and regional testing of our children. By the time these students become high school juniors and seniors, I have observed them in the struggle to excel and grasp the material that will help them prepare for adulthood. In my opinion, we are steering away from the core principles that influence personal growth and development. Thus, I believe urban schools are shifting into a testing center rather than becoming an environment that will groom children to serve a valuable purpose in life.

Career Exploration. Goals that you have set in regards to exploring your career interests and that may also lead to long-term employment are considered career exploration goals. Career exploration includes planning for post-secondary education opportunities; volunteer work associated with exposure to your career interest(s); and seeking internships that provide practical experience.

Living in the inner-city of a metropolitan region in the United States had become a completely new experience for me. For the first time in my life, I realized that not every person grows up learning the value of labor and service. In addition, I learned the unfortunate ripple effect of youth going through a weakened education system; they become less prepared to enter the workforce or post-secondary learning opportunities. Communities that experience generations of this unintentional systematic process, families then become limited with financial resources, skills, and other important factors that strengthen the family dynamics and encourage personal growth.

The more I have become exposed to this new life, since I was about ten or eleven years of age, I witnessed how people spent their days deprived of resources and opportunities to experience a decent lifestyle. Throughout my teen years, I heard most of my peers stress the need for and desire to earn an income to help support their family or to provide for their personal needs and desires. Part of the reason for this occurrence has been because families experience significant droughts without relevant resources and a lack of financial support to maintain their livelihood. Depending on how you are raised and where you are from, you may assume the question, "why are children starting to feel responsible for their family when they should focus on their education and enjoy their youth?"

Job Placement/Employment. The truth to the above matter is that children are trying to *earn* their advantage to break a cycle, but what really happens is that by "jumping the gun" they "kill" their advantage before they get a chance to create one. I say this because from a youth perspective, teenagers associate their quality of life with their financial resources and to gain financial resources you must have a job to earn them. By using the S.M.A.R.T. Goal Planning process, you will discover a healthy approach to the job search and employment seeking process, so that all able persons can earn the opportunity to meet their needs and elevate their competence. This leads into the reason I have defined job placement and employment seeking as finding and securing an opportunity for gaining income or to build upon compensated work experience.

Financial. The discussion about job searching and employment seeking leads us into our last goal focus, which is financial. Financial goals include the basic principles of financial management allowing us to explore concepts to manage, increase, save, or invest monetary resources to support our basic living needs and educational expenses. It is important to understand proper handling of financial assets, but it is just as important to learn how to earn and attract the funds.

The Planning Process

The S.M.A.R.T. Goal Planning process is designed to guide anyone through the planning phase of goal setting. Typically, if you are setting a goal you will identify what you are aiming to do, then determine how you want to document or establish this goal. Furthermore, you may create a few objectives that can measure your progression, but the adversities you will encounter along the way will impact your desire to pursue the goal. One of the many factors that prevent or delay a person's willingness to pursue something is the feeling of being overwhelmed with the unforeseen factors that get in the way. The five parts of the S.M.A.R.T. Goal Planning process are meant to ease some of these overwhelming factors by asking questions to help you elaborate on the details that may often get overlooked in the process. This process can shape your perspective and open your eyes to see a clearer vision of the direction that is best suited for you to explore.

The first part of the process is to identify the type of goal that you will pursue. You can easily have multiple goals, but it will serve you best to have them each outlined with a clear understanding of the variables that can potentially influence your progression. So, use each section to guide you as you attempt to outline the important details about your goal.

Specify. In this section of the planning process, you will clarify some details to help you develop a clear and vivid understanding about your goal. You will need to provide a precise description or statement of the goal. Next, you will describe the impact this goal will have on you, such as the sacrifices you will need to make and the potential benefits you may receive. Then, determine how this goal will prepare you for future opportunities.

Measure. Once you have specified the goal, here you will determine the method(s) to use for tracking your progress.

Measuring your goal is assessing the progression you have toward achieving it. Create a list of tasks that are necessary for you to complete and that will move you closer to the finish line. In addition, write down some examples of natural occurrences that may hint you are on the right track. For instance, compliments and other acknowledgements are considered natural occurrences. Goals that are measurable are more likely to be attainable.

*A*ccess. Pursuing a goal will require a certain amount of assets and resources. Depending on your financial status, awareness, and abilities, you may have access to certain resources that are not easily accessible to others. Having access to resources can make the world of a difference for you, especially, if these items can be obtained and properly used. The purpose of this section is to become more aware of the assets and resources that are readily accessible to you based on proximity, affordability, and your competence.

*R*ely. Every success story and every successful person has hardly ever been described to have gone solo. I say this to inform you that success is rarely accomplished by one person or measured by one event. Success is a dependent that relies on you and others that you involve in your circle to support and motivate you to achieve your goals. Success becomes owned by the individual that inputs a significant amount of effort, but gives credit to everyone that is involved. Therefore, you should always identify the individuals that rely on you to succeed; the circumstances that are changeable based on what you can achieve; and the support you have in the process to help you reach your destiny.

Time Frame. We only have 24 hours in a day, which is equivalent to 1,440 minutes that we must use each day. When we subtract no more than 8 hours of sleep, we take away 480 minutes and are left with 960 minutes to be productive. Time is precious and should be used with much caution because each moment we spend uses up valuable time that could be used to empower greatness and blessings upon our life. We all have a lifetime to manage, but there is no guarantee for how long we shall live to manage it. For this reason, many goals have an expiration or due in season; their season may only be opportune for several days, months or even a couple of years. Beyond this time frame your chance to reach a goal may become more challenging or implausible. Once you set a goal for yourself, allot a period that is reasonable for you to maximize your time to pursue your aspiration.

Plan Execution

Once you have gathered all the details about the goal you are about to pursue, now it is time to put some action behind the idea and the plan. You can only have a fair chance to discover your destiny when you execute your plan. So, what does this mean for you? Just because you outlined the details of your goal and thought deeply about what it will take for you to reach your destiny, it does not mean you are ready. There are some preliminary action steps to help you move along on this journey. Your goal is like a vision, you see it first, now you must go backwards and look at the small things you must do to get there. I am going to give you some basic steps to help you get a head start, but after these steps it will be up to you to figure out the rest.

Step One: Prepare Yourself for the Journey

Think about this opportunity like you would a vacation. What are your necessities? What are your essentials? When you prepare to travel, you pack mostly for where you are going and not for what you will go through to get there. In other words, think about what you will need once you have achieved your goal. What kind of image must you have to hold a Bachelor's Degree or maintain employment? What kind of skills do you need to be that successful engineer …doctor …lawyer, and so on. So, before you do anything you must work on yourself, first, to be prepared for your destiny. This is very important because you want to be able to manage your blessing when you receive it, so that you can cherish and maintain it much longer. I'm sure you have heard of the saying, "practice makes perfect," well this is exactly one of the points I am making when I suggest and urge you to prepare yourself for the goal you are about to achieve.

This journey you are preparing for will require you to increase your knowledge and awareness. You will need to sharpen and develop more skills. You will need access to resources. Depending on your goal, you just might need to seek more opportunities. These are just a few of the practical ways to consider and to adequately help you prepare for this journey.

Step Two: Identify the Routes to Travel

As you can probably recall, someone in your life may have said these words either directly to you or indirectly when speaking to another person, "...there is always more than one way to get things done." When considering the path that you want to take to accomplish a goal, you must acknowledge and admit to yourself there is more than one way to reach it. This is often difficult to do for some individuals because you generally spend a lot of time meditating and planning how you want or imagine your dreams to play out. Other individuals have difficulty knowing what to hope for as it concerns themselves and their futures. Then you have the people that are accustom to someone else planning their life based on traditions or expectations. With many things to consider, regardless of the circumstance that fits you, you can only focus on the things you can control. For instance, if you are planning to travel to a place that is more than six hours away, the first decision you will contemplate is how will you get there? What may determine your choice is what you can afford to spend. In addition, you should consider your personal limitations outside of cost, which may include physical capacity, health conditions and the state of others who may travel along with you.

So, in a like manner, when you are about to execute your plan, you should be aware of the controllable elements and the variable conditions that exist. Anything that is in your realm of control make sure you understand their significance and the impact of those elements because they may be vital to your position to reach success. A few elements that are controllable include your behavior, attitude, appearance, character, actions, thoughts, and social engagement. There are probably more elements than those listed that you can control, but I do not want to overwhelm you with a long list of them. I shared the few that are pivotal, so you can begin to go in the right direction.

Another aspect of determining the route you will take is the experience you would like to have. To emphasize this point, I want to exaggerate the concept in a real-life experiment.

Microwave vs. Oven. For the purposes of this exercise take a homemade meal and reheat a portion in the microwave and another portion in the oven at 350 degrees. Once they have been heated enough to eat take your bites and make a note on how each meal tastes.

Hopefully, we have come to the same conclusion. Although oven heated meals are slower to warm up, they can retain more of the original flavors and textures than microwave meals. In context, when you consider the experience that you want to have, determine whether you would like to travel the long way or the short way; are you in a hurry or can you take your time to reach your destination. If you would like to know the truth, when it comes to success there is no such thing as a shortcut because everything about success requires a process. The process that you need to endure has many things for you to learn and skills for you to develop, which will eventually help you maintain what you may achieve. Success that matures over time is authentic and sustainable, whereas, success that happens quicker than the usual process does not last as long. These moments can create what I like to call fabricated success. Fabricated success is like the "get rich quick schemes." It may give you the rewards, but you will lose the growth, maturity, mental capacity, and many other essential elements that will help you to sustain the magnitude of your achievement.

Step Three: Pack up and Go

Here you are... after meditating on what you need... after considering the path you want to take, you are finally ready to get this show on the road. This step is so critical because you do not want to spend a whole lot of time trying to plan the perfect trip because accidents will happen and unknown circumstances will arise. So only consider the essentials, the things that matter most and what you can control. Have your main contacts for support, hop on this adventure and JUST GO!

Principle #4: Let God Take You There

A man's heart plans his way, But the Lord directs his steps. (Proverbs 16:9 NKJV)

There are many plans in a man's heart, Nevertheless the Lord's counsel—that will stand. (Proverbs 19:21 NKJV)

You will have many ideas flowing through your mind. You may even figure out how you will bring those ideas to fruition. Then you go through the process of developing a plan that you will later execute to see what you have envisioned become a reality. So, like most of us, you forgot the most important component to include in your plan, the "But God..." Factor. We can get so caught up in what we believe we can do for ourselves that we lose sight that the only way we _are able_, is because God, our Creator, made it possible for us to _be able_. Even with our own abilities, some circumstances may seem impossible for us to resolve or overcome, but we are constantly reminded that God can make the impossible possible. (i.e. read Exodus 14:21; Matthew 28:5-7; John 12:1; Acts 13:30.) In addition, the areas where we lack, God makes provision for us to have enough, especially when our money gets funny and resources seem low. (i.e. read 1 Corinthians 3:7) Our abilities are granted to us for seasons with a purpose to bless others and honor Him in our lives. So, these abilities are never permanent. (i.e. read Psalms 75:7; Romans 12:3-8) And, when we think we are alone and can get away with things, God is aware of every action and covenant made, in which He will hold us accountable to each of them.

Throughout my life, it has been evident that having support, resources, and accountability encourages you to become confident that your goals are possible to obtain. The intention of this modified model is to organize the resources that are accessible and establish a strategy for the best approach that will help you reach your goal. The plan itself organizes the details for your strategic approach by identifying important factors that are needed to improve your chance to achieve your goal.

The foundation of any goal starts with the person that hopes to establish them, in this case, that is YOU! In the next chapter, we will discuss more about the elements that are included in the makeup of this foundation. You will learn how to develop a foundation that will position you to act upon your planned approach. The foundation, as it will be later described, identifies several factors to support the stability of your efforts to pursue your aspirations.

Chapter Three
The Success Platform

When you begin to create success, you must understand that your success will only last if your foundation can sustain itself against all pressures. Since we are talking about a concept that is only realized and not something you can put your hands on, what could possibly be the foundation of your success? Well, if you have not guessed it already, your success starts with YOU!

You are the primary and common factor in determining the success that you hope to achieve. In order to position yourself so that you can improve your chance of reaching your goals, you must learn the areas or elements that are pivotal to your personal growth. I have identified five prime factors of personal growth that also contribute to your ability to succeed. These are the five elements that create the success platform,

1. Social & Professional Imagery
2. Resume Building Techniques
3. Personal Assets (Resources & Skills)
4. Social Groups & Networking
5. Financial Stewardship

These elements or categories have a significant influence on a person's growth and development. You, for instance, can use these areas to self-evaluate or assess your strengths and weaknesses. Each element has a set of skills, which you will develop and improve upon, so you can use them to advance and explore opportunities. With these set of skills, the success platform illustrates the core values for developing a culture of success. It is important to identify these foundational elements with a culture because if these categories are valued and considered a growth priority, the individual will have an increasing chance or show a rich history of reaching goals and succeeding in their endeavors.

BUILD A FOUNDATION

> *"When the whirlwind passes by, the wicked is no more,*
> *But the righteous has an everlasting foundation."*
> *(Proverbs 10:25 NKJV)*

A foundation is the starting point of anything that is intended to grow, develop, or be improved. In context, the foundation is one of the most important components to be established first. The foundation is the platform that contains the substance required to sustain what is being created or manifested. For instance, kindergarten is the grade level where children learn the fundamentals of cognition, social engagement, and independence. Before any athlete begins training or the learning of technical skills for their sport, they must prepare their mind and body for those skills through a period of fitness training, called conditioning. Even prior to performing technical skills athletes continue to condition themselves, but with less intensity. Furthermore, a foundation is by way of preparing for or creating conditions necessary to manifest the outcomes intended.

ALL YOU NEED IS THREE

> *"Though one may be overpowered by another, two can withstand him. And a threefold cord is not quickly broken." (Ecclesiastes 4:12 NKJV)*

It is often suggested in many areas that three is your prime number, not because it can only be divided by itself and "1," but rather it has carried significant meaning in theology, geometry, writing, engineering, architecture, public speaking, and many other disciplines. As a prime number, in this context, three symbolizes strength, stability, and balance. In terms of building a foundation for pursuing goals, I would like to explain how "three" is significant in this process. The success platform consists of five elements that every person should develop periodically throughout their lifetime. As it relates to an individual's goal, at least three of those elements will be essential, if not necessary, for a person to use so he or she can progress forward toward the completion of tasks or accomplishing the goal itself. It will not be uncommon for someone to find a way to utilize all five elements, but I assure that three of the five will be used predominantly. In this instance three is taking on the properties as if it were being used in architecture or engineering disciplines. Having three personal elements used to pursue a goal builds confidence (strength) so the individual will stay in pursuit of his or her goal. The three elements also provide a degree of support (stability) allowing for an individual to bear the pressures or overcome obstacles that may arise along this journey. Last, but not least, three elements fairly distribute (balance) the use of a person's strengths to advance closer to his or her goal.

DEVELOP A CULTURE

> *Imitate me, just as I also imitate Christ. Now I praise you, brethren, that you remember me in all things and keep the traditions just as I delivered them to you. But I want you to know that the head of every man is Christ, the head of woman is man, and the head of Christ is God. (1 Corinthians 11:1-3 NKJV)*

A culture, as I would describe it in addition to the traditional definition, is a set of habits or methods that are transferable through natural inheritance or succession. Traditionally, culture is spoken in relation to a person's heritage, background, or the traditions passed on to generations to preserve their history. Many establishments use this term when they are interested in maintaining standards, quality of service, and other attributes that contribute to their level of success and growth. Most often these groups try to simplify methods so that new hires or promoted employees can adopt skills, work habits, and techniques to perform their responsibilities at an expected level.

The foundational elements of a culture are standards, core values and principles. These elements create expectations for the people that agree and believe in those concepts. If an expectation is not met, the consequences that follow enforces accountability, responsibility, and encourages effort. In addition, these three elements provide us with the ABC's for creating a culture of success. First, develop standards, which are based on someone's *ability*, whether that individual is aware of them. Standards are used as measures or guidelines to encourage performance and enforce the execution of certain actions. Next, identify core values that are aligned with someone's *belief system* connecting them to a purpose. Core values indirectly maintains accountability by initiating an internal desire for a person to remain true to themselves and uphold an authentic sense of character. Then, instill principles, through *concepts,* based on truths or proven theories, that produce intended results. The concepts should influence actions that resemble the core values and uphold the given standards. The idea behind creating a culture is all about developing a system that is adoptable by any individual that decides to accept the *"terms and conditions."*

LEAVE A LEGACY

> *"Every place that the sole of your foot will tread upon I have given you... as I was with Moses, so I will be with you. I will not leave you nor forsake you. Be strong and of good courage... Only be strong and very courageous, that you may observe to do according to the law... that you may prosper wherever you go. ...For then you will make your way prosperous, and then you will have good success." (Joshua 1:3; 5-8 NKJV)*

A legacy is defined as monetary possessions or property that is passed on to someone. Growing up having something to pass down to younger generations was a huge deal in my family. My grandparents and their siblings were constantly talking to me about how one day I will be able to continue various things that either they or my parents have started. But as I walked in the footsteps of my father, I realized that what is left behind is not always tangible. My parents were nowhere near rich or wealthy, but they are great in character, they're smart and wonderful in other areas. From kindergarten to sixth grade, an expectation was placed on me before I even stepped foot into a classroom. In those same years, when I played recreational sports there was a performance standard that was expected of me because my father had a great athletic reputation in the community.

The early years of my childhood showed me that we have more to pass down to our children besides the wealth of money and material possessions. We have knowledge, skills, wisdom, experience and so much more that we can give to the next generation through our social DNA. Your social DNA is comprised of habits and personal traits that are transferable through engagement, observation, and the teaching of beliefs and principles.

Like-minded people that share a belief system, principles, concepts, lifestyles, and other customs create a culture. Most cultures pass down social structure, characteristics, history, and a wealth of knowledge so the upcoming generations can withhold the integrity of a family and the culture, itself. In addition, the culture itself can grow or evolve with the advances of society without compromising the core values. This holds merit with people who value and have obtained some degree of success. The methods and paths people choose to accomplish their goals may vary, but the core principles and type of resources used remain the same. The five elements described earlier are the core elements that I have identified to remain consistent among successful people and they are like pillars of a strong structure that I depend on whenever I aim to reach a goal. Therefore, creating a culture of success is the best way to develop a legacy for your family, your business, our education system, and any other infrastructure with a system of inheritance.

Principle #5: Live with Purpose, Intentionally

But Daniel purposed in his heart that he would not defile himself with the portion of the king's delicacies, nor with the wine which he drank; therefore, he requested of the chief of the eunuchs that he might not defile himself. (Daniel 1:8 NKJV)

Therefore, whether you eat or drink, or whatever you do, do all to the glory of God. (1 Corinthians 10:31 NKJV)

And whatever you do, do it heartily, as to the Lord and not to men, knowing that from the Lord you will receive the reward of the inheritance; for you serve the Lord Christ. But he who does wrong will be repaid for what he has done, and there is no partiality. (Colossians 3:23-25 NKJV)

If you decide to live for something or someone other than yourself, you will be encouraged to live by higher standards with new expectations out of life. The things that you would have done for your own satisfaction or considered to be acceptable per your standards, will no longer become an option. Ultimately, I am encouraging you to live for God and believe in Jesus Christ because He is the Light in your darkness, the Way to your destiny, and the Word that gave YOU Life. So, I challenge you to take the first step of welcoming Him into your life by dedicating your life to *willfully do* for others, as it is "...your reasonable service." (Romans 12:1 NKJV)

Chapter Four
SOCIAL & PROFESSIONAL IMAGERY

When you are preparing for an interview or meeting someone for the first time, they say, "dress to impress." Also, there is a saying that, "your first impression is your last impression." Both statements express that your initial presentation of yourself will influence how people choose to remember you. In addition, these concepts may also imply that you only have ONE chance to take advantage of any opportunity. If you only have ONE chance that means you must practice and be near perfect. When I think back on the times when adults would encourage me with these common quotes, I did feel a lot of pressure. Sometimes, I even thought that the way I prepared myself was not enough. Eventually, this motivated me to become competitive in almost every aspect of my life because I knew that there was a chance someone else may be better than me or have some favorable advantage over me. Although I was young and felt all this pressure to work toward perfection, I matured with a mentality that I can always get better and make improvements.

Hearing how important it was to present myself in my best appearance and with my best attitude and behavior, I began to think and wonder… "Why are they emphasizing this if I am only a kid?" "I know that *practice makes perfect*,' but does it matter to me at this point?" Now that I look back at those moments, I realized that it was part of a process for me to develop into the person I have become. Believe it or not, my elders and other adults were indirectly teaching me that if I looked my best and behaved at my best, I will have a chance at better opportunities. Also, they were teaching me that conducting yourself with good behavior and appropriate mannerisms is a sign of self-respect, therefore, it would be likely that others would respect you as well. These concepts may have been explained to me when I was a young boy, but I did not understand them. Once I became a little older and understood the history behind what my elders and other adults believed or experienced, then things started to make more sense. At this point, I was a teenager that finally figured out that the way we dress, how we behave, and what we say are all components of our image.

Your image has a significant impact on the opportunities you can receive, along with, the relationships that you choose to develop. Your image is your brand... Your image is how people recognize you. Your image tells your story... Your image sets the foundation of the legacy you will leave behind on earth... Your image is your life!

When you go to the grocery store, do you buy based on the value, the quality, or the brand of the product? Some people choose a combination of these methods just to get the better deal. The value of a product is deemed reasonable if the price can be paid. The quality has significance if personal needs are being met. The brand gives credit to the reputation that the product has among its consumers. Likewise, **we have value**, **we are significant**, and **we are reputable** based on the lifestyle habits we develop over time.

Your value and self-worth are associated with your ability to meet the needs of others that can afford what you can offer. Whereas, your reputation is built by the way you consistently conduct yourself around others, which holds merit to your character. Individually, we have the choice to hold ourselves to the standards that we create. In addition, we can also choose whether we want to exceed those standards. Standards are expectations that justify what you believe by holding you accountable to the principles that represent your beliefs. A standard is like the minimum amount owed on a credit bill, it will keep you committed to your responsibility and only require a minimum effort to apply certain skills and knowledge to a situation.

The worthiness of your abilities determines the value of your support and engagement with others. Learning how to interact with others in all environments is a skill within itself that attributes to the development of qualities that distinguishes you from everyone else. There are several components that create these distinctions and once you develop constant behaviors and actions, then you will begin to establish the kind of person you are likely to grow into.

Principle #6: Discover Your True Self

We live in a world full of diversity, which could present itself as a challenge for some people, especially if you do not understand how you may fit in the mix. Your roles, abilities, heritage, and purpose contribute to your personal identity. For many years, it has been common for individuals to become identified by their associations - parents, siblings, friends, organizations, institutions, and other affiliates. For instance, in the past even centuries ago, people were often identified by the expression of whose child they were, the street they lived on, the city they resided in, and the peers they associated with. In my opinion, this way of identifying yourself does not seem to be embarrassing nor negative, rather it helps people understand and learn a little bit about you and your roots. Your place of origin is not always a physical place, but in general, a place where you learn and grow, which allows people to assess your potential. Usually, your parents, your family, and the environments, which you may often become exposed to, are your primary influences that you will learn from and adopt your habits and behaviors. The characteristic traits and other attributes that are developed from such exposure may help you to coexist among people and adapt to your environment.

It seems like the youth growing up in today's diverse society are striving to create identities that are appealing for social engagement, rather than seeking to learn who they are born to become and understand what their purpose is for their lifetime. Self-identity used to be a topic concerning people that sincerely desired to discover their potential, family heritage, and purpose for living. Nowadays, I often question whether the intent to discover one's true self is about personal development or to create a personality or persona that is accepted by peer groups and society. I believe our self is divided into two beings that coexist for us to live on Earth - Spiritual and Human natures.

"And the Lord God formed man of the dust of the ground, and breathed into his nostrils the breath of life; and man became a living being." (Genesis 2:7 NKJV)

Therefore the general origin of who we are is derived from the God that created us. Nonetheless, the process of His characteristics being passed on to us is replicated when we have children of our own, being born in the likeness and image of their birth parents. This is important because if we learn about God, as well as our parents, we can create a foundational understanding of who we are and what potential exist within ourselves. Although, genetically and spiritually, we possess the potential, we also are given the independence to determine how we will grow from our known point of origin. The decisions we make, our behaviors and the way we process information, all contribute to the individual we will eventually become.

Knowing who you are and whose you are will have the greatest impact on your life more than anything else. You may have thought you read the previous statement wrong, but you didn't. I had said, "whose you are" because knowing who you belong to will help you to define your roots, both physically and spiritually. These two phrases "who you are" and "whose

you are" associates you with the roles that are inherently assigned to you with a special intent. Roles give you responsibility and that responsibility will help to define your purpose.

Let us further breakdown, in detail, what makes up your image. I have divided the concept of "image" (which can be applied to any individual or establishment) into three components: (1) Expressive (2) Physical (3) Qualities. Each component is an aspect to the concept of an image and for each aspect there are two characteristics that describe the function of each component. Before explaining each component remember **all three** aspects and the **six characteristics**, *together*, are part of **ONE** image, thus producing a brand. So, there is no way to separate a person's image or a brand because all parts are a representation of YOU!

Expressive

When you are expressive, you are opening the door to the innermost part of yourself, which can be considered a sacred part of who you are. This also puts you in a vulnerable position and can often feel uncomfortable. A position of vulnerability means that you are allowing yourself to share something you value, believe, or possess with someone else, hoping they will receive what you have shared with sincere understanding. In addition, you may try to establish a sense of trust when you share sensitive information.

Therefore, in any instance that you may need to be expressive or share information about yourself to someone, it is very important that you learn how to communicate with clarity and understanding. Your ability to express yourself involves how well you can convey your thoughts, feelings, emotions, ideas, and other messages to people. For you to become an effective communicator, you should learn how to use different methods of communication and appropriate language.

Communication

Communication can be generally defined as the way in which signs, symbols, sound, gestures, and other transmitted signals (communicators) are relayed to compose a message. Here, in the definition itself, you can see that there are many ways that you can choose to deliver a message. The method that you use should be understood by the person(s) that are receiving your message. For example, if you are a parent of a preschool age child you will not try to write a message to him or her, rather you would speak to them using words and a tone of voice that will help them understand what you are saying. This example is really the best way to describe how to become an effective communicator. If you apply this to a profession, you can still figure out that communication methods, tone of voice, and gestures are important for developing a sense of clarity in your discussion. Doctors, lawyers, social service professionals, teachers, administrators, and executives all have a unique way of communicating within their respective work environments. If either of these professions were asked to talk to someone who is not familiar with the lingo they use among their colleagues, I am sure that they would adjust their language for the "outsider" to comprehend what they need to say.

Language

Language has a significant function in being expressive; it is a way of communication that is systematic, using a specific method or usage of communicators. Language can be specific to a culture, nation, community, professional industry, or society. We have many different languages and dialects to those languages, which makes our world such a unique place to explore. You can speak the same language, but if you travel to a different region some terms and the way people sound will be much different from your own. When you are exploring new places, it is best to get familiar with the people of the areas that you visit, so you can learn their method of communication.

All of this is important to learn. You must become aware of what you express to others as you engage them in different places and environments. Your actions, behaviors, and gestures all communicate a message, but each situation can influence what each of those may mean. So, as you encounter other people in different environments, be conscious of what you say, how you say it, what you do, and your intention for the engagement. Someone can easily misinterpret your expression, which may result in you not receiving the response you had anticipated.

Physical

There is an old and very common saying, "don't judge a book by its cover." This is commonly used when someone is encouraging another person to avoid making assumptions about something without prior knowledge. Although we try and try again to avoid having pre-judgmental thoughts, we have them anyway. These thoughts are pre-conceived from circumstances that you may have experienced or observed in the past. So, in a way, you are not judging a person by their circumstances, but rather you are referencing from your past and associating that with their current situation. The same concept is valid when you evaluate an individual either by his or her appearance or behavior. Different characteristics can tell you a lot about a person, but only if you are interested in knowing more about them beyond what you see.

Appearance

Let's define *appearance* simply as the physical attribute of **appeal** or **attraction** based on what someone can see. Sounds simple, right? Well, it is. Your appearance should be intentional, especially, when you are in public or professional environments. Before leaving your home, try to anticipate what you want others to say about you when they take a quick glance. Being a little conscious of what others may say or think should be encouraging to you when you are preparing for the day. My grandparents always told me, or at least hinted, that when I go to school, to a performance, or any place of importance I should dress and look my best because, "you never know who is out there watching you." Wake up in the morning with the intention not to be impressive, but to become a better person by caring about how you appear to others. If you only "dress to impress," it can become exhausting, but if the impression that you give is your natural self, you will shine in every environment that embraces your presence. Being fashionable is not necessarily how well you can adopt to the most recent and modern trends, but rather how you can connect with who you are to what you want others to grasp from your outward appearance.

Presentation

The second characteristic of the physical aspect is your presentation. Presentation is like your appearance, but we are going to describe it as the *demeanor, attitude, delivery, display*, or the *way* someone or something is shown in an environment. A person's appearance is mostly connected to fashion, but their presentation is solely about how their intention and purpose is demonstrated. Although, your appearance may be the same as you transition from one place to another, your presentation will be different, depending on your purpose for being in that area. Now, take a moment to imagine yourself at home as you are about to relax. Then, imagine yourself at school in a classroom or at your workplace trying to relax. In these scenarios, let us assume you were wearing the same thing at home as you were in public. Would you say, the way you tried to relax in either environment will be the same? I think not! This was my example of demonstrating how your appearance can be the same in different places, while your presentation changes as you transition and adapt to the conditions of each environment. The condition of your environment will always have an influence on how you decide to conduct yourself. The unforeseen or unnoticeable moods can alter these conditions you feel from others in the area. In addition, you may become affected by the physical arrangement of a space. Also, your state of mind can impact how you feel about being where you are.

Avoiding environmental disruptions requires **focus;** keeping a positive state of mind, followed by positive behaviors, and a few more actions. This, in fact, is crucial because you want to make sure your conduct compliments your appearance. You might ask, how would you do this? Well consider this, would you wear a tuxedo or a ballroom dress to a wrestling match? Probably not. You must be conscious of the activities you are engaged in, so that you can concentrate on having the right approach. Try considering the atmosphere of the environment before you get there. Is it formal or informal? Is this a place to be social or professional? Are you going for work or at your leisure? Think about it as if you were playing a sport. Is what you are doing comparable to a championship game, a regular season match-up, preseason exhibition, or are you still in practice? I compared an environment's atmosphere to sports because each type of atmosphere is different and requires a different kind of presentation.

- <u>Practice</u> - An environment with a "practice" atmosphere your appearance is not at all important, but rather **your potential to learn and demonstrate ability** is priority.

- <u>Preseason Exhibition</u> - An environment with a "preseason exhibition" atmosphere **execution** is the primary focus; but you are also expected to appear as though you would in a real match-up.

- Regular Season Match-up - An environment with a "regular season" atmosphere **requires** that your <u>presentation</u> and <u>appearance</u> are **both** treated equally as important when you are **executing your efforts.**

- Post-Season/Championship - An environment with a "post-season or championship" atmosphere you are expected to exceed your normal expectations and execute **better than your best** effort.

Qualities

The third aspect of image is qualities, which is a little more challenging to describe. Qualities involve characteristics that define the kind of person you portray to be toward others, as well as, yourself. These characteristics identify growth, personal development, interests, and preferences. I firmly believe that a person can have good and bad qualities, with the majority having the greater influence on your outcomes as you progress in life. In addition to the other characteristics we have covered - communication, language, appearance, and presentation; now, we are going to discuss the icing on the cake, your personality and character. These two characteristics will describe the unique aspects of who you are. By learning your preferences and other ways to describe yourself, you will discover that your beliefs, morals, and values have a major impact on the personal qualities you will develop over time. It is essential that you become centered and grounded with a *reliable* belief system, *ethical* principles, and *core* values.

Personality

Your personality involves how your thoughts, feelings, and behaviors combined influence your actions, choices, habits, and character. Your personality is made up of many characteristics that attribute to the way you think, feel, and behave. These characteristics are developed through your beliefs, which are connected to your personal morals and values. Having a unique set of characteristics and preferences is what forms an individual's distinctive character. In the Jungian Type Inventory, there are four sets of preferences that create 16 personality types. You can discover your personality type by using the Myers-Briggs Type Inventory. By taking a Myers-Briggs personality type assessment you will learn your dominant personality type which helps to describe both your mentality and the role that, presumably, best fits you, naturally.

Character

Character describes actions and the dominant role you have throughout your life. Similar to a movie, your character is developed by your purpose, thus, originating from your morals and values. According to your belief system, you may be expected to handle situations and respond to circumstances with certain actions, intentions, and mindset. Responding, repeatedly in this manner, will create an instinctive response and before you know it, you would have adopted this habit into your lifestyle. As a result, your character can be described as the mental, moral, and behavioral qualities that define you as an individual.

Image Types

When you read a novel or story you read from the writer's point of view. A writer can tell their story as a narrator in third person or as a character in second or first person. Your life is a story that has already been written, from the moment you took your first breath, until you exhale for the very last time. People can observe your life through the image that you portray. The life you live is only seen *at a glance* by other people, but with a perspective that has a limited truth to the reality that you experience. Once all truths are put together, you can get a better glimpse of who you are in this *live* story. Every person is represented by three versions of themselves

- *personal*, *professional*, and *public*. Each version describes a different persona and gives insight into that person's life. Regardless of your persona, people should be able to say things about you that are consistent across each version that will reflect the basis of your true character.

I have learned that when we are young, we will try to develop characteristics that other people desire for us to have. In doing so, we fabricate an image that will satisfy others, but will leave some of us with discomfort, confusion, and uncertainty. Then, once we get older and learn more about our feelings, thoughts, and behaviors, we recognize that what we **truly** desired for ourselves is contrary to what we have been living out over a significant period of time.

Look at yourself in the mirror when you are in your room, the bathroom, your car, and even at work or school. What do you see? If I'm correct you see yourself, you may have different clothes on or facial expressions, but nonetheless you see much of the same features in all mirrors. These three versions of your image are just like mirrors. Each type reflects YOU, but with a few differences because of the environment they are associated with. We will explore these image types to clarify how they represent who you are.

Personal. The personal image type is a self-reflection or perception that is revealed to others based on what someone shares about themselves. Basically, it is how you describe yourself to others. Your personal image is mostly all of what you know to be true or factual about yourself and the way you express those characteristics when you engage with other people. In addition, your personal image is also influenced by the beliefs and moral standards that you have accepted to develop your lifestyle.

Professional. The professional image reflects someone in a work or professional environment, revealed through the person's conduct and work ethics. Often your professionalism is shown in environments that demand discipline, respect, time management, polished appearance, perfection, and execution with your best efforts. There is a common quote which says, "you are a product of your environment." It is quite possible for our environment to have an influence on our personal development. But, we also have a choice to either conform to our surroundings or to become better than what we have seen around us. An environment can encourage you to adopt a set of standards that will create adaptable habits or help you to develop your lifestyle. If you accept these standards, they will help you to blend in or set yourself apart from others. Regardless of where you started or how you grew up, those environments that you have been exposed to taught you something about your connection to your surroundings.

Public. The public image is the common knowledge understood by others about a person. I often consider the public image as either the residue left behind or the shadow of someone's presence. In this context, your *residue* is the mark left behind when you allow yourself to be remembered by a person, group, or community through your words and actions. The shadow of someone's presence is closely related to branding because it resembles the outermost elements of your image without the defining details. A *shadow* is a silhouette of an object or person when light shines upon them. You leave a shadow of your image when you impact the life of others, while you are present. Whenever we have an encounter with someone or a group of people, we can impact their lives with our words and actions. If the impact you have on someone becomes influential, then you have a higher chance for that person to share positive characteristics about you with another person. Now this person only knows the highlights about you through the words of those that you have impacted.

Use and Function

A person's image is so dynamic that it serves many purposes, yet functions differently depending on how it is used. For instance, when you attend an interview for a new opportunity, your image is being evaluated to determine if you are qualified for that experience. Furthermore, if you are developing a new relationship with someone, your image becomes the measure of compatibility, so either of you can decide how to pursue the relationship moving forward. The essential point is that your image will always become a factor when you engage with other people.

People engage with one another for either casual or formal reasons. Casual engagement is common for socializing or entertainment. Formal engagement is often associated with institutional learning, employment, and other professional interests. People do not always engage socially for *just* entertainment, but often to learn something significant. When people observe one another to learn how to adapt in a new environment or how to interact with different people that is called *socialization*. Socialization is a hidden process that occurs when a person desires to become more aware of the conduct that is socially accepted. Socialization is a continual process that a person experiences to acquire their identity from learning the social norms, values, behaviors, and skills appropriate for his or her social position.

When you interact with people on the job or in other professional environments, it is possible for you to develop personal and social relationships. This is even true when you interact with classmates or peers in an educational environment. In fact, some employers and institutions create an atmosphere that encourage positive social engagement, but their aim is to develop cooperation among the people hoping to maintain or improve productivity. Formal environments, such as school and work, encourage different forms of engagement among their people for many reasons; but primarily to create an atmosphere that helps everyone serve their purpose. Your ability to balance and separate your social and professional relationships is a skill that demonstrates your *professionalism*. Professionalism is having the competence or skills that are expected of you to execute your role.

After discovering all that you can about yourself guided by this breakdown of your image, I can only assure you that there will always be room for you to become a better person. Have an open mind toward life, other people, and the goals that you want to achieve, while staying grounded with good standards and values. An open-minded person is not someone who accepts anything, but is a person that is willing to understand with a little optimism at times. You are an individual of great value and someone in this world is waiting for you to share your worthiness with them. So, do not be shy, all the time, allow other people to see and know your worthiness and humbled character. Everyone may not accept who you are or the value you may bring into their life, but anyone who embraces the man or woman you have become will receive a gift and a blessing. Before we move on, remember to pursue life with a purpose and live each moment with appreciation.

Chapter Five
BUILD UP YOUR RESUME

The Inspiration That Lies Within...

When you are out looking for a job, employers often request that you have a resume. Upon graduation of high school, it is part of senior seminar that you learn how to create and format a resume. For those students who are and parents that keep their children advanced beyond their peers, resume building starts before the paper is formatted and filled with content. Resume building starts with skill development, knowledge bearing, talent execution, and sincere efforts to help others without the expectation of compensation in return.

Today, in our modern society, job placement and employment seeking has become more competitive than ever before. This is true not because there are a lot of seasoned and young candidates competing for similar jobs, but rather people competing against a machine. As time passed, decade after decade, skilled labor has become more technical reducing the amount of talent required to fulfill the need of laboring positions. So, if skilled labor is not in demand as much, then what is? Service! Customer Service, Indirect and Direct Sales, Marketing, Management, and any role that involves engaging with people. When the job opportunities change and industries shift to become more technologically advanced, this directly affects the living conditions of individuals that depend on their skills to take care of their family. So, what happens next? Our education system begins to adjust their curriculum by shifting teaching methods and learning objectives with the changes that occur in the workforce.

Public education has altered drastically since I was in grade school. I remember being in school and computers had been introduced as a tool for learning. It wasn't common then for households to have a computer, but somehow my family had one. This gave me an advantage over my peers because I was fortunate enough to study and learn advanced concepts outside of the classroom. The lessons and assignments that my parents and grandparents were unable to help me with, the Berenstain Bears, Mavis Beacon, and Vtech were there to catch me in my struggles. Little did I know, these small introductions to modern technology began to prepare me for the new generation of employment, while my grandparents were slowly being transitioned out of work and my parents were being forced to keep up with the technology. Although computers were stepping in, I still had a chance to experience learning in a more traditional manner, especially with teachers that did not allow us to depend on technological resources. I can honestly say this made a difference in what I understand now about education and becoming successful in my life.

Children are learning more from computers, while the demands of local and state government pressure teachers to meet new standards almost every year. With our public education system experiencing so many changes to how children are required to learn *just* the basics, I hear more declining results in academic performance than ever before. These changes are occurring in both the inner-city and suburban neighborhoods. Some of the core fundamentals are being extracted from what children should learn, like spelling. Although, we have spelling and grammar correction functions embedded in computers these skills are vital for basic communication. As a result, how can the next generation become prepared for service positions if they are not able to learn how to communicate properly? The skills of the next generation are going to require that young people learn skills of independent learning to fill-in the gaps of the traditional public education.

Not only has the changes in our education system affected the learning of our youth, but also the household structure and family dynamics have had a significant impact on the growth and development of people from infancy on through adulthood. Think for minute about your upbringing and childhood experience until you became a mature adult, not the legal age of adulthood. Some of you reading this may think to yourself you are still growing and have yet become a mature and wise adult; this is exactly my point. Children that grow up in broken families and without the knowledge or even the awareness to know their parents, they may struggle for at least the first 18 years navigating through life. For some children, they struggle trying to figure out why traditional school is so important, if they already feel empty on the inside.

It appears we hardly pay attention to these details when considering how a person prepares and decides to pursue any form of employment, whether it is paid or volunteer. Lately, I have encountered teenagers seeking job opportunities more than finding help to succeed in school. When I say succeed, I am not referring to the kind of success that requires honor or merit roll, I just mean at least pass academically with a "C" average or above. In addition, parents have been more concerned with their children taking responsibility for their own education and finding a job, but less often have I encountered parents desiring to strengthen their relationship with their children. Some parents honestly want to have a healthy relationship, but the dynamics of their living circumstances create barriers that impact the mental health of most families that struggle to maintain their livelihood.

At the end of the day, the people that are competing for employment are individuals aiming to improve their living conditions, so that they can provide the basic needs for their family. Our young people struggle to find employment, simply because they are unprepared - not equipped with skills, lack discipline and inspiration, and have not developed the mental capacity to handle responsibility. I say this, not to disrespect their youthfulness nor to disregard any barriers in their upbringing, but to bring awareness to parents, the community, the Church, and employers that we need to take better care of our children, if we expect them to take care of us when we need them in our later years.

By now you probably forgot we were discussing resume building techniques... LOL!

Well, all the above matters when we discuss how to build and create the contents of a resume. The entire purpose of a resume is to give an employer or colleague a glimpse of your professional background. Your resume can tell a story about the path you are on to reach your destiny and to fulfill your purpose. Therefore, realize that there is more to the story besides what is written on a piece of paper. A significant amount of your work ethics and skills are developed from home rather than by formal learning and training. Parents, as well as other individuals, that take part in raising children should and must encourage work ethics, responsibility, and accountability through chores and other reasonable household duties. Eventually, children will learn how to (1) respect authority, (2) make an earnest effort to complete tasks or assignments, (3) accept responsibility, especially after making any kind of mistake, and (4) value the rewards given after a job well done. These concepts are reinforced with formal systems, such as school and the workforce, which also can help to broaden your awareness of future opportunities, if you continue to develop good work ethics and skills. For these reasons, I find it necessary to understand how your life experiences, blended with your professional development, can prepare you for job opportunities and future career paths. Now we are ready to explore the fundamentals of a resume, how a resume can be used, and what strategies should be considered to improve your chances to become a worthy candidate for professional advancement.

Principle #7: Prepare to Be Chosen

But the Lord said to Samuel, "Do not look at his appearance or at his physical stature, because I have refused him. For the Lord does not see as man sees; for man looks at the outward appearance, but the Lord looks at the heart." (1 Samuel 16:7 NKJV)

Do not anticipate being chosen for an opportunity, just choose to be a qualified individual. I encourage you to position yourself for opportunities that will help you grow and mature into a responsible person. Opportunities are best chosen when you decide how you will benefit from the experience. Early in your career exploration, you should consider opportunities that have the potential to impact your personal growth as well as your professional development. You will always encounter different kinds of opportunities for you to pursue, but every so often, choose opportunities that will help you develop positive characteristics and qualities that may help you in a future experience. Most opportunities, whether it is for employment, education, entertainment, empowerment, or your enjoyment, have a criteria or standard for you to qualify, or as some may say, "to get your foot in the door." When you are considered for an opportunity it is *assumed* that you have met or exceeded the minimal requirements. Whereas, if you are chosen, it is *proven* that you possess and demonstrate the ability to honor the valued experience.

Here are three steps to help you prepare for any opportunity.

1. Learn the requirements - the needs, preferences, and abilities.

2. Identify someone that is suitable to coach or mentor you for the opportunity.

3. Find other opportunities that will offer a chance to develop the areas you need to strengthen or improve upon, for you to adequately meet the qualifications.

Resume Fundamentals

A resume is a document that lists and organizes a person's work history, educational background, and other information that can help someone qualify for employment or other opportunities. However, a resume is a tactical resource, often used to secure employment that will provide a person with their basic needs. On the other hand, the components of a resume can help the individual prepare for opportunities before that person is ready to pursue them. By learning the different parts of a resume, you can assume that your experiences will not only extract your interests, talents, and abilities, but also put you in position to reach your aspirations. Therefore, giving our youth an early introduction about resumes and how they are used as a tool for advancement should help to prepare teenagers and young adults for the workforce.

In the past, it was common for someone to learn about resumes in an English Language Arts class, a resume writing workshop, or a seminar course. Now we have YouTube, webinars, online courses, websites, and applications on computers and mobile devices that can guide us through the process of creating a resume. Resumes have many sections that can describe your professional capacity. Employers want to see that you can commit to responsibility, execute tasks, learn when an opportunity presents itself, and add value to their organization with experience, skills, and other abilities. Your resume should be a direct reflection of your current capacity to handle such roles and duties. Each section that can go on a resume is important, but only necessary for roles that benefit from the content related to that section. The various sections of a resume allude to the areas that may need further development to polish your presentation for future opportunities. The main sections to include on your resume are the education, work history, and skills sections. These are the standard sections that are generally included on most resumes, but depending on the industry there may be other areas that are important to include, as well.

Given that there are many sections of a resume that may provide good content to describe a person's professional capacity, the time it takes to develop skills, obtain knowledge, and gain experience has a significant impact on the individual's preparedness. When building your resume, you must take the time to grow in the areas where you need improvement as well as exercise the skills that are your strength. You may consider taking a course, or attending a workshop, or watching an instructional video to explore the areas that you have identified for improvement. The most important reason to give attention to those areas is for your own personal and professional growth. Furthermore, exercise your stronger skills by exploring ways to use them. There are volunteer opportunities, community service projects, relatives, friends, and neighbors that could use your abilities in some capacity. Stretch yourself, just enough, so that you do not let your skills become dull. In addition, you want to keep yourself refreshed with knowledge, wisdom, and skills in areas that hold your interest because technology will always advance faster than we can keep up with it. Even if you are not actively or using your abilities on a consistent basis, at some point, your untapped or underused ability may benefit you in the near future. For example, when I attended Horizon Science Academy, in Cleveland, Ohio during 7th grade, I learned advanced technological skills such as how to build and repair computers and how to develop websites. With either the skill or knowledge, I did not see an immediate use for them. But, during my years in high school I used these skills to help older adults, especially senior citizens, learn how to use computers. Also, I performed basic computer repairs and upgrades for Windows users, as well as, designed websites for people with their own business. By doing this, I was able to earn a little income during high school and throughout my years in college. You can never know, for sure, which skills that you possess will become an opportunity, unless you find creative ways to use them.

Employers may not consider "time" in the same manner that I have described, but it is a factor in their decision to hire a candidate. Employers look at the gaps in your employment history; they want to understand the relevance of your education; and how you have applied your skills listed to the various roles you've identified. Regardless, if you are a student in high school, college, or even graduate school, consider your employment to be a practical learning experience.

How to Use a Resume

Resumes are often submitted with job applications and used to create profiles for job search engines. Resumes are important when you want to advance in a career, or seek meaningful employment, or find a job to maintain your livelihood. In addition, I have found an even more valuable use for a resume, it helps a person fulfill their purpose. This may be difficult for some people to grasp and understand how a resume has this kind of impact, especially, if it is only known to be a record of the things *you have done* or accomplished. The phrase "you have done" implies that you made a choice to pursue what you have experienced. Some people *only* receive minimum wage jobs because they choose to pursue what is available in the moment. Low paying jobs are good for individuals that are starting out in the workforce or for people that look for an immediate cash flow. Others, who are skillful and talented, that settle for low paying jobs may not believe that they have the skill capacity to receive or handle a higher paying job. There are also low-income families that are fearful to let go of the benefits from government assistance. Either way every person is given the power to make choices that will influence their future.

There are many examples where people choose to reduce their standards or make decisions based on what seems to be the easiest. The essential point is that a person's mindset must be renewed with new ideas, principles, and beliefs that support a mentality of a new standard. Your commitment to these new concepts will produce actions that demonstrate your acceptance to a new standard or mentality. Eventually, you will transform your mindset and become an example to others that wish to follow. Therefore, everyone has choices to make that will influence how they will experience life. Each choice opens a gate to a path that will, hopefully, lead you to your destiny.

Improve Employment Opportunities

The content on your resume has a very important role in helping employers evaluate your potential for the applied position. The content you choose to include on your resume must be strategically applied in each section. For this reason, it is important that you carefully consider the opportunities you decide to experience. Sometimes, to gain valuable experience, you will need to volunteer, participate in community service projects, or create an opportunity to develop certain skills.

The average person will almost and always apply for those opportunities that are available with tasks that seem easy or simple to perform. There is a fair chance that you gain valuable experience using this method. But, you can gain even more experiences by challenging yourself to explore opportunities that will require you to learn new skills. The mindset you have going into the job searching process will influence how you decide which opportunities are suitable for you. Situations and circumstances are also key factors that affect the way a person weighs their employment options. Considering all factors, making decisions for how you will pursue opportunities is not as easy as it may seem. Learning how to assess your needs, your interests, and your abilities, within reason, will help you to make short-term and long-term decisions.

Understanding what circumstances require a short-term versus a long-term resolution is based on the need level and how it impacts your living conditions. For example, having little food in the home versus not having transportation, how would you evaluate the level of need? Which of the situations would you determine needs a short-term or long-term resolution? Now, with the same two scenarios, consider the following circumstances:

A. You are single with no children;

B. You are a single parent of two children;

C. You are single paying child support;

D. You live with your significant other with no children;

E. You live with your significant other with at least two children.

With these examples, you can see how circumstances can change the way you view your choices.

Tending to your needs is necessary and should always be a priority. Once your immediate needs have been met, think about a long-term need that you can work on. Often needs require skills and financial resources. Needs are different than goals. Needs are imperative to a person's livelihood and goals are tailored to a person's interests. Resumes can be used to meet a need or satisfy an interest. For you to improve your resume, you should know and be aware of what you are pursuing.

When you are physically and mentally prepared to work, you should explore opportunities to learn your interests, desires, and needs for self-gratification. Personal gratification can influence your thoughts and perceptions. Discover and learn about the things that intrigue your growth and spark your desire. Ideally, you should want to use your youthful years to explore and learn practical skills and gain valuable knowledge. Then, use your later years to build upon your experiences, receive the benefits, and enjoy your life.

Improving your employment opportunities starts with identifying your drivers - your needs and your personal interests. Next, assess your experience to determine whether you have enough to pursue future opportunities. If not, you should seek activities, programs, trainings, and other practical learning opportunities to develop more skills and the right experience. If you need professional or personal development, find something that is conducive to your current schedule and make sure you can find the most affordable, if not FREE, opportunities. Remember, cater your time to address short-term needs as your higher priority. In addition, let your imagination explore the possible ways you can utilizing modern resources such as the Internet, eBooks, YouTube, or even online courses.

I hope you have learned that a resume is more than a document that describes professional readiness and experience. Resumes are tools that individuals can use for professional advancement, job placement, and assessment of their professional capacity.

Chapter Six
It's All About Growth

The Inspiration That Lies Within...

Every one of us has been given breath, a chance to live, and an opportunity to nurture and edify the world that we live in. In addition to our roles and responsibilities, we are bestowed with natural talent that should be used to fulfill a specific purpose. Our natural roles define our purpose, the gifts that we possess give us value, and the needs of others determine our worth.

Growing up as a child, I thought my worth would be determined by my future career and that people would notice my value through my material possessions. I thought this was true because movies, magazines and other media outlets displayed wealth based on monetary value or materialistic worth. But, as I matured and became exposed to other truths, I realized that the worth of our material possessions are, indeed, associated with a monetary value. On the other hand, our individual worth is determined by the usefulness of our knowledge, skills, and other abilities to help and support one another. When you begin to associate a monetary value to an individual, you are almost declaring that the person can be bought or exchanged for something of "equal" value. In this case, people would begin to undermine the purpose of humanity and individuals will later lose sight of each other's worthiness, seeing one another to be disposable (i.e. only useful for a personal need or desire).

Once you realize that your purpose on Earth is worth more than the things you desire, you will be able to discover the greatness that already exist inside of you. Each person has their own combination of skills, characteristics, strengths, and other abilities that make them unique. An individual's uniqueness can give them a distinct advantage over others, as well as, help to fulfill a meaningful purpose in life. Although the uniqueness of who you are is made up of many characteristics and a combination of specific abilities, each one of those traits and skills are developed over time. Therefore, you should nurture each trait and ability through your experience, exposure, and exploration. As you continue to grow and mature, you will become a better person today than you were yesterday.

Your personal identity and your professional brand are created by the image you develop as you grow and mature. You will always have an opinion about yourself, but to effectively evaluate your characteristics, you will need support from others. How can you find the right people or person to help you evaluate yourself? First, I will suggest that you assess your current, but closely developed, relationships with the people you often encounter in different environments (i.e. domestic, academic, professional, and social). Allow these people to describe who you are to them and identify any potential strengths and weaknesses that they notice when you are in their presence. Select people that you believe can share their honest opinions about you, even if it may trigger your emotions a bit. People that meet this criteria are the best *critics* to help you during your self-assessment.

Growth & Development Opportunities

Everyone has the potential to become better individuals by improving personal attributes and advancing their skills and knowledge. Our potential exists because we were already given the tools that we need to demonstrate our worthiness in this lifetime. We all have personal assets that are essential to our individual growth and these assets may also help with the fulfillment of our purpose. If we are blind to our most valued possessions, then life becomes a challenge when we find ourselves experiencing moments of defeat. Sometimes when we feel defeated it is not because we are unable to overcome the challenge or obstacle, but more so, we are unaware of how we may overcome them. Therefore, it is necessary for you to learn how to identify your personal assets, so that you can:

1. be aware of the tools you are equipped with to fulfill your purpose and reach other goals;

2. have a way to evaluate your strengths and weaknesses; and

3. develop areas that are influential to your personal and professional growth.

Sometimes the goals you desire may seem a little beyond your reach, but it is possible to obtain them. First, think about the steps that it will take for you to reach your desired goals. Next, consider the actions that will be required of you to complete each step. After that, identify your assets that may be helpful during each step as you strive to complete them. Your personal assets are resources, qualities, characteristics, and abilities that allow you to navigate through, cope with, and develop from the experiences you encounter in life. Personal assets are used to improve your chances to become successful and reach your goals. We are going to group them into the categories, tangible and intangible. If you are not familiar with these terms, keep in mind that tangible assets are those items and possessions that you can put your hands on, whereas intangible assets are things that do not have physical properties to be touched.

Identifying Assets

Tangible Assets. Generally, people can identify physical things that can help them complete a task or accomplish a goal. Nowadays, these possessions are essential for convenience, preference, or fashion. Years ago, when I was in school to complete a research paper or book report I needed encyclopedias, World Books, almanacs, and the library, but today I can go on the Internet and search websites for information. Talk about convenience, technology has made information more accessible to grasp and allows learning to occur more frequently. In order to access the Internet, you will need either a computer, cellular phone, or some other kind of mobile device that will connect to the Internet. In the past, success was mostly reached by manual labor, which require 100% or more effort from individuals.

In our modern day, we have the support of technology that performs most of the work for us, which allows us to reach our intended outcomes much faster than before. The problem with people today is that new generations are being born in a "microwave" era and speed is of the essence. "The faster the better..." "Rather sooner than later..." "Hustle up or get passed up..." These are all phrases that seem inspirational and encouraging, but they give people a misconception about what is truly expected of them. Although these phrases are intended to create a sense of urgency within the "heart of a person's will," people can easily become discouraged. I know that some people feel doubtful about their performance meeting specific standards. Also, workloads can feel intimidating or too intense for some individuals, while others with an entrepreneurial mindset, may view work intensity as an opportunity to develop an alternative method that will reduce physical labor.

Tangible assets are meant to enhance our ability to perform rather than replace our capability to execute tasks. Therefore, learning and being conscious of the older methods to perform tasks are just as important as being skilled in the modern ways. Be aware of the items you possess, knowing their intended functions and extended uses.

Intangible Assets. Quite often, we underestimate the value of our natural talents, developed skills, gifted abilities, and the knowledge we obtain. These assets cannot be grasped, but when executed they are well observed, which makes them intangible. If someone were to ask you to evaluate all your personal assets, what would be your first response? Probably, something you can put your hands on. Any person, including myself, would have considered a similar initial response. Why? Well that's a good question. When you evaluate how you will assemble a piece of furniture that you just bought, will you think about whether you have enough experience or would you simply search for the instructions to put it together? Precisely, you will find the instructions and consider the physical tools required to help you assemble the furniture. Let's get a little abstract. When a four or five-year-old starts school, do they consider their mental capacity before entering a classroom? Or, do they simply trust in their parent(s) or guardian by obeying their instructions to behave and listen to the adult that will be watching over them? You guessed it right, they will do their best to listen and follow those instructions to the best of their ability. Typically, any person will choose to rely on their strengths or what they feel is most dependable, especially when identifying personal attributes.

When a person seeks to pursue a goal, it will seem easier to seek out the How-To instructions rather than try to figure out the best approach that will require more effort. The How-To instructions provide the step-by-step guidance, which keeps you focused on completing each task. Afterwards, you may dwell on the possible fact that you either learned a new skill or figured out a new use for a skill that you already had. This goes to show you that, sometimes, our intangibles are just an afterthought, only because we do not pay much attention to their significance. Imagine, if we were taught early on that tools for learning included the ability to comprehend and interpret? You said it, we would be like, WHAT? or HUH? The process of learning develops these innate abilities, but until you develop a consciousness to value the process of learning these intangible abilities are just the natural result of human development, repetitious habits, or intentional practice.

We do not discover, soon enough, the value of our intangibles. It takes a while for some individuals to realize the importance and significance of an ability; but I can honestly say once we make this discovery, it has the power to alter how we perceive ourselves. Intangible assets are very essential for our personal growth and advancing our abilities to experience life in different capacities.

Evaluate All Aspects of Self

There is not one person, except for Jesus Christ, that I know to have lived a perfect and righteous life. Even though we are not perfect, we can perfect areas that need some improvement. In some instances, we could correct some of our mistakes. When you correct a mistake, it does not undo your actions nor your decisions, but it may validate a lesson that you should have learned. A second chance only allows you to make a better or wiser choice than what you have made in the past.

There are some people that have the desire to discover how they can become a better person. If you are one of them, I recommend that you, first, learn and explore the different methods to evaluate your personal characteristics. Through this process, you will discover your dominant personality, preferred learning style, common behavior patterns, and many other characteristics that describe your uniqueness. The purpose of a self-assessment is to help you identify, both, strengths and weaknesses that present an opportunity for future growth and development. As you put forth effort to make personal improvements, keep in mind that you can always enhance a strength and a weakness has the potential to become a strength. However, strengths are only as strong as the need for them to be utilized, while weaknesses are underutilized abilities that have not been exercised as much. Take a moment to think about why some people are lefties, righties, or ambidextrous. People have different levels of dominance when it comes to the use of their symmetric body parts. (i.e. arms, hands, legs, etc.) Whichever side is used the most becomes the dominant side, whereas, the other side that is used the least acts more like an aide, to guide or support. Individuals that are ambidextrous have the advantage of equal dominance, allowing a person to use either side based on their preference or the circumstance. This example best describes how to understand your strengths and weaknesses, so that they both can be valued. If this is your first time going through a self-assessment, take a moment to discover the facts about yourself first. Regardless of your age, gender, and abilities, if you do not understand who you are, it will become difficult to grasp the meaning of the characteristics that identify with you. Once you learn general things about yourself, you should notice themes in your life that may lead you to the discovery of your purpose.

Before learning about how to assess yourself, you are probably wondering how do you go about the self-discovery process? Well, this is where the rubber meets the road. Self-discovery and self-assessments measure different aspects of how you present yourself to others. If you recall in chapter four, we discussed the three aspects of your image; the two functions of your image; and that your image describes only one YOU. The process of self-discovery is identifying the primary characteristics, behaviors, and trends that best describe the kind of individual YOU portray in public and in private settings. Consistencies that are found in both public and private settings may be considered your dominant characteristics that create your image or branded identity. The differences that appear between both settings are either necessary for a role; required for engagement; or newly developed behaviors or characteristics. Self-assessments will help you identify skills, characteristics, knowledge, and other abilities that you possess. These identified abilities can also be aligned with your goals to help you develop strategies and recognize opportunities that may help in the process of pursuing those goals.

Sometimes you may not even recognize that the opportunity for you to achieve your goal is dependent upon an ability you have not bothered to nurture or develop. This seems to be common among several people that I have encountered. Some would admit that an underdeveloped skill or ability is the reason they have not achieved what they have hoped to accomplish. While others are unaware that they have the capability to reach their desired goals. If these people would have stretched themselves beyond their comfort zone and spent some time to build upon their untapped talents, they just may have had a chance to explore new opportunities.

The process of evaluating yourself is such a humbling experience. It also heightens your awareness of your actions, choices, behaviors, thoughts, and habits that subsequently develop and improve your sense of accountability to pursue dreams, desires, and goals. In addition, I have learned that *lack of accountability* can hinder your growth because you will start to blame other people and things for your short comings.

Stretch Yourself

It is important that you connect and engage with people that can challenge you because challenges help you grow. You should not want or desire to be the best individual among any group because that will encourage complacency. This is not to say, do not have people around you that may not be as good as you, but keep some diversity among your associations. Allow yourself to be stretched; stretched beyond your comfort zone and into a territory that will nurture growth and expand your horizons. We all have a lifetime to manage, but there is no guarantee for how long we will live, so why not explore the unknown and discover opportunities that await your arrival?

Take heed to wisdom, adhere to the authorities that preside over you, because your life is too precious and you deserve to live for a purpose and not for the correction of your mistakes and mishaps. Although, you may be doing well and you are potentially in a good place in your life, there is still room for growth. Complacency will hinder you from experiencing and receiving the abundance of blessings that have been promised to you, many years before your time. Therefore, no one person should settle for where they are in life, but desire and yearn for more... yearn for the treasures that you have yet to embrace. The treasures, in reference, are much more valuable than the cars, homes, jewelry, stones, money, and other materialistic possessions. The treasures I reference are those things that no one can take from you because they dwell within you - love, joy, peace, longsuffering, kindness, goodness, faithfulness, gentleness, and self-control. You may recognize these as the "Fruit of the Spirit," these are the ultimate treasures that we need to strive after. When a person chooses to make the conscious effort to reach and maintain this level of success, they decide to live a life of complete prosperity in its full capacity.

Personal and professional growth occurs from learned experiences that trigger a need for change from the inside out. True growth begins with self, then it manifests outwardly in the behaviors and actions displayed. Any person can learn a lesson and apply the knowledge gained to a situation, but not all people make a commitment to change a lifestyle, so that they can improve their quality of life. So, get the best from your life by living for reasons greater than your own pleasures. Do not grow up thinking that the world can revolve around you, but rather believe you can resolve issues around the world. Think beyond yourself and find ways to extend a hand to others because the life you once lived, someone else is living it.

Principle #8: Acknowledge Your Blessings

Every good gift and every perfect gift is from above, and comes down from the Father of lights, with whom there is no variation or shadow of turning.
(James 1:17 NKJV)

Once a year in America, we celebrate the season of thanksgiving with family, friends, loved ones, coworkers, and classmates. During this season, people will openly share their gratitude for one another and appreciation for opportunities experienced or things they have obtained in that year. No longer do I feel the desire to wait until the end of the year to express my gratitude for all my blessings, instead, I believe we should give sincere thanks for all that is given to us throughout the course of the year.

There are many kinds of blessings that we should learn to appreciate, rather than advocating for the things we desire. Blessings are meant to enhance and bring well-being in the form of favor, provision, and protection. We should honor the basic blessings that we are given each day and for every moment we can live with ample food, shelter, clothing, and a sense of security.

Let no one seek his own, but each one the other's well-being. (1 Corinthians 10:24 NKJV)

Therefore comfort each other and edify one another, just as you also are doing. (1 Thessalonians 5:11 NKJV)

As you learn how to appreciate what you have, value relationships with people that have a positive influence on your life. Express your gratitude and thanksgiving, not only, with your words, but also, with your actions. Showing your appreciation is more than just saying, "Thank You!" It is also shown through your gestures, generosity, servitude, and attitude. All that you possess and the people you are connected to appear in your life for a reason, showing your gratefulness is the least you can do. After all, your success will begin with what you have because what you do have is enough to help you reach your destiny.

Chapter Seven

UNDERSTANDING YOUR CONNECTIVITY

The Inspiration That Lies Within...

"It's not what you know, but who you know" that will get you ahead in life. I have honestly heard this expression more times than I can count, but in my experience, life has validated this partial truth. Yes, I consider this a part of the whole truth, because my reality has shown me that with both knowledge and ability paired with a network of supportive people, there is hardly anything that can get in the way of you and your destiny. It is very important to assess the company that you wish to keep because they can have a subtle influence on you, depending on how close you become and the depth of your relationship. Relationships that you have had or will develop are very important and should be examined carefully. I have learned over the years that building relationships is an essential part of my success, but coincidentally, I recognize that building relationships is an area that I also need to improve upon.

When I decide to connect with people, I do so with good intentions, pursuing each relationship with a purpose. I am not a social butterfly, but I do get a chance to engage with family and friends for personal enjoyment and social activities. During the early years of my childhood, I did experience some special moments with my parents, grandparents, aunts, uncles, and cousins. I spent so much time visiting family members that I rarely stayed in one place where I could settle in my own bed. For several years, I shared rooms, slept on pallets (i.e. layers of sheets and comforters to sleep on), and traveled from one house to another with a backpack or suitcase with my clothes, a blanket, and my favorite pillow (or pillowcase). I guess you could say, before cellular phones, tablets, and PDA's, I had already adapted to a mobile and compact lifestyle.

At this point in my life, as a kid, I was unable to truly understand how to develop strong relationships, even with my own family, except for a few cousins that I grew up with that were like my brothers or sisters. I stayed in touch with a few cousins up until I was about ten years of age. We would exchange weekend visits staying overnight at each other's home, traveled together, and became a part of one another's life like siblings. I also had a few peers that I considered to be "my friends." As a kid, I considered my friends to be individuals that I spent most of my social time talking to, playing with, and even visiting for a duration of time within a day.

As I approached ten years old, I saw these relationships beginning to fade as things began to suddenly change. My mom decided that my younger brother and I were both going to move in with her fiancée and his son, who happened to be a few years younger than myself, but older than my little brother. For the years that I spent in kindergarten on through 5th grade, I periodically stayed overnight at my maternal and paternal grandparents' home. I was very uncomfortable with making this change to live with my mom and her fiancée. This kind of change in my living situation was not the first time I had lived with my mom and another man that was not my father. At first, I was a bit skeptical because I had previously stayed with my mother while she had been married to my brother's father. That experience was interesting, to say the least, and I had been exposed to the inner-city lifestyle for the first time, as I was about five years of age.

I said "inner-city lifestyle" because environmentally the suburban area and inner-city are like night and day. In the 1990's, places like Warrensville Heights, Bedford, Shaker Heights, Pepper Pike, Maple Heights and Solon were areas that the working-class (middle-class) families lived. I feel that my exposure at a young age to different lifestyles was very broad, but having to adapt and live in a new environment was a challenged. Therefore, specifying the environment and my age should help you to grasp the kind of mentality I was in, let alone the emotions I may have felt.

Now that I was about ten years old meeting my mom's fiancée for the first time and seeing that he lived in the inner-city, I began to become concerned about the distance away from my family and friends.

Living in Warrensville Heights in the 1990's, I was only minutes away from my immediate family and other relatives. My friends were all in proximity to my grandparents' homes. If I were to ask whether I could visit a relative or friend, usually, that request would be granted if it was within reason. But, now living at least a 20-minute drive away from them, I figured my visiting days would be cut to a minimum. Not only that, I figured it would be just a matter of time before I am presented with the idea to attend a school that was in a convenient location, closer to the home where my mother and her fiancée lived. This transition was going to be the hardest of all because now relationships that I had developed were either coming to an end, a pause, or a break-up. This included friendships, companionships, teacher-student bonds, and other relationships. This was a very difficult moment in my childhood because it felt like my life was starting all over. I spent a few days saddened and trying to understand what would happen if I lost those relationships. Now, thanks to social media, I can stay connected with some of those people, but being so young at that time, things just didn't make sense.

The transition from living with my grandparents to living with my mom and complete "strangers" was not as bad as I had probably imagined. It was indeed a process to get through because my lifestyle had to change, there were new rules to follow, and my neighborhood was not as friendly nor trustworthy compared to where I came from. Before, I completely moved in with my mom and her fiancée, I could alternate between my grandparents' homes, while I attended lower-middle school for 5th and 6th grade. After a while, the traveling for both my mom and her fiancée became stressful to transport me back and forth, as it also became a challenge for my grandparents and my father.

The time came, when I was about to enter 7th grade at Warrensville Heights Middle School, my mom had arranged an appointment for me to interview and take an entry exam to see if I qualified to enroll at Horizon Science Academy in Cleveland, Ohio. My original plan was to intentionally fail the test, so I can remain with my friends in Warrensville Heights just a little while longer. My friends and I had plans to play on several athletic teams together and really compete in organized sports. Although this was the idea, my mother had her own agenda. She had brought with her everything she had that could possibly display how I performed academically - awards, transcript, recommendation letters, etc. After the Dean of Students reviewed my documents, the next question he asked my mother was, "When would you like for him to start, tomorrow or Monday?" You had better believe I felt disappointed, in other words, I was "salty." I looked at my mother and was hoping for her to at least reply, "Monday," so I could say goodbye to my friends.

The next day, Friday, was an emotional day for me, I sat in all my classes and for the first time in my academic history I didn't care to do any work. I laid my head down and just meditated on the things that had occurred during the year. The one event that affected me the most was the accident that took the life of my cousin, Terrance Johnson, on April 1, 2001. He was like an older brother and always took an interest to be around and care for me when he could. One year in elementary school, when no one at home was available to stay until it was time for me to walk to the bus stop, my cousin Terry, faithfully, drove over each morning to make sure I got to the corner to catch the bus safely. There were so many things that Terry did for me that I will never forget and always appreciate. As I continued to ponder about the past, I just thought about how I will leave some valuable relationships, including both family and friends, that I felt were very important in my life.

Although, I dreaded the transition to a new school, I am glad that I did attend Horizon Science Academy for the following three years. The Dean of Students made sure the science, mathematics, and technology teachers pushed me beyond my limits and helped me to reveal some hidden gifts I didn't know I had. I thought the only subject I enjoyed was math, but with a STEM focus, Horizon Science Academy showed me how these subjects were relative to everyday living practices. The school demographics was culturally diverse, the student population was small, most of the STEM teachers were from Turkey, and the school was in an old office building previously occupied by AAA. The school was new to the area and had only been open for one year. The international teachers were not easy to understand at first, nor was their writing clear to read when copying my notes from the board for class. This was the first time I was in a mixed learning environment with students of other races, nationalities, and other cultural differences. The only way I cared to make friends was by competing on the basketball court. I remember the first time I stepped foot on the basketball court and it was by chance. As I waited for my ride, one of the 8th graders had to leave during a 5-on-5 full court game, so his team picked me up. Once I touched the ball for the first time… let's just say I became noticed by the "popular kids."

Academically, my only challenge was dealing with the stereotypes that some teachers had on students, specifically African American boys. I came from a predominantly African American school district, which had been considerably rated for good performance in the State of Ohio. Apparently, I was not accustomed to this attitude; I felt like this was the first time I experienced a taste of discrimination. I remember one of my teachers gave me an "F" in her class, I clearly completed assignments and did well on my exams. My work had been re-evaluated and that "F" was no more. I give thanks to my mom for supporting me and the Dean of Students for investigating. At this point, I didn't know who to trust at school, nor was I completely comfortable with my new living arrangements, which I knew would be for the next several years, at least until I graduated high school.

As years gone by, I didn't develop many solid relationships. I mainly engaged with my peers at school or on the phone. Some I interacted with through sports, but I really did not get to know them. One of the reasons was simply because, unlike my peers in Warrensville Heights, these individuals lived nowhere near me and I already knew my mom and her fiancée were not interested in using their gas to let me go visit a schoolmate. Therefore, I basically isolated myself from the idea that I could develop any kind of meaningful relationship with anyone at school. This inspired my interest to just get the best out of my academic experience, where I knew I had been bound to excel. The administration of the school was very interested in my scholastics, which led them to identify me among a few other students, as a school leader or ambassador. In this role, we all were like the model scholars that Horizon Science Academy wanted to develop and send off to some of the top colleges in the United States or even the world.

Being a top scholar for Horizon Science Academy, at this stage in their development, allowed for us to explore field trips, special projects, experiments, abroad traveling experiences, and other exposure opportunities. Along with this recognition, there were many challenges that followed. I could randomly get pulled out of class for any reason by the Dean or teacher that was among the leadership of the school. Quite often, I received last minute parental approval for various opportunities, which normally resulted in calling my mom, while she was at work. Regardless of the circumstance, I was still responsible for learning the lessons that my teachers taught during regular class time and completing the assignments on time. There were some instances where I may have been given an extension, but it was within a reasonable period to match the length of time that my classmates had to work on special assignments. Eventually, I found out that most of my teachers agreed that I had been learning at a level beyond most of my classmates. This presented opportunity for me to become an independent learner, basically a candidate for independent study, only for certain circumstances. During my independent learning experience, my teachers and administrators had an opportunity to learn more about me as a student and an individual, in return, I did learn more about them as well.

Here, I would like to give credit to my K-6th grade teachers of the Warrensville Heights School District that taught me between the years, 1994-2001. I credit them because they had always pushed me to strive for excellence in everything that I put my mind and heart toward. For this reason, I have chosen to never give up nor settle for any effort that is less than my best. There was a tradition in Warrensville Heights to sign your peer's student planner when they were transferring out of the district. I had carried my Warrensville Heights planner most of the time during my 7th grade year at Horizon Science Academy. When I found myself feeling alone, momentarily, I would glance at a few pages and be inspired by the comments my friends wrote about me. Some of my peers that wrote in my book shared some heartfelt comments that often brought me to tears.

Before I transitioned out of Horizon Science Academy to move on to Glenville High School, my competitiveness led me to be academically ranked #2 in my class holding the same GPA as my classmate Seana. I found out that she only had the #1 rank because her last name began with an "L" which comes before my last name, which starts with an "M". I had a lot of respect for her, because although I did not get a chance to know her well, I observed her habits and she put in the time and effort to reach the level of success that she had back then and probably has now in her professional career. Now that I have overcame the challenges that I encountered when I arrived at Horizon Science Academy, I developed the faith that I can do better than my best effort.

If I had been doing so well at Horizon Science Academy, what brought about the need to transfer schools? Well, outside of my academics, I was also known to be a pretty good athlete. Since the school did not have neither middle nor high school sports, except for a newborn basketball team, I played for recreational teams. I had played basketball for both Kovacic and Thurgood Marshall recreation centers. In addition, I played in the Cleveland Muny Football League for the East 88th Street Browns and the E.M.S. Rams Youth Football Team. After my first year with the East 88th Street Browns, my stepfather started the E.M.S. Rams. I had a dual role in this process, first I started the youth executive board that was tasked with developing community relationships and fundraising activities for the team. Once the time came for the season to start, I became the leader for all divisions - midgets, peewees, and bantam weights. Throughout the organization's development, I gained professional exposure to community related issues regarding youth, education, poverty, and other activism topics.

During the season, my speed and athleticism, in the quarterback and safety positions, attracted the attention from several high schools in Cleveland, one was Glenville High School. My second-year coach for the Rams, was familiar with the football program at Glenville, which some of our new plays modelled to adapt to the fast talent on our team. Somehow, the quarterback coach for Glenville High School began giving me private lessons for a few weeks on how to develop several basic quarterback techniques for me to execute the new plays I had to learn. Their QB coach was impressed with my ability to learn quickly and how I had improved my throwing accuracy that he, eventually, suggested I was ready for high school football. We were about to start the season for Muny League and my team was counting on me, so I decided to remain until the end of the season. I was also thinking that I would have to transfer yet again leaving relationships that I was beginning to develop at Horizon Science Academy. Following the football season, I managed to make the junior varsity and varsity basketball team for the second time. In the previous year, I could not stay on the team because my stepfather was unable to drive the distance to the west side to pick me up from practice. But this year, practice moved from the west side to Kovacic Recreation Center, which was closer to the school. The first game or two I had a rough start and ended up getting dropped from the starting lineup and became the 6th man. Nevertheless, I turned up the heat by the third game against Max Hayes High School. With my defense, forcing turnovers and my ability to capitalize from our opponent's errors and score, I could lead the team to a victory as well as earn my position back as a starter! From that point forward, I became one of the star players and a team captain. I believe I was already emotionally disturbed at the fact that I was going to have one year playing with friends that I developed a chemistry with outside on the basketball court, where we played all year-round. Nonetheless after my freshman year, I left another group of friends behind to move onto a new journey in a new environment.

If you followed Cleveland's local news in 2004, you would remember that Glenville's athletic programs had been all over the news headlines. But, even the greatness of the sport programs did not substitute for the academics that the school lacked. In all fairness, in my opinion, the teachers were not the issue, the public education system had been compromised. When I transferred into the Cleveland Municipal School District, I had been informed by my counselor that many of the courses were removed from the curriculum due to a deficit. While the football team was making history on the field, I started my own in the classroom. I did not have an official class schedule for about six weeks because my counselor was having a difficult time transferring my credits from Horizon Science Academy. The courses that I had taken were advanced and certainly not equivalent to any courses available in the district that I could receive credit for at Glenville High School. As you can imagine, I was not happy about this situation. My concern was more about how colleges would view my transcript without knowing the true story. I accepted the circumstance for what it was and I knew trying to transfer back to Horizon Science Academy was not an option. It was until one week before the quarter was over that I received my real schedule for the year. Unfortunately, I was new to the classes and I had about six weeks of assignments, tests, and quizzes to make up in three honors classes and physical education. You are probably thinking what I thought, "how in the world will this be possible?" Well let me tell you, I aced all my classes by the end of the first quarter, finishing with a GPA of 4.7, which became the highest grade point average among all students in all grade levels.

I was so surprised at the result of my performance for that one week that I silently wondered, "how could this be?" How could I be this advanced beyond my peers? I had never earned a GPA so high where the next person was at least 0.5 points away from my grade point average. I, eventually, shared the news with my mother and suggested to her that I would prefer to take college courses. I knew about the Post-Secondary Options Program at Cleveland State University because Horizon Science Academy took college-bound students on a field trip and the tour guide shared how advanced students could enroll in college courses as early as the ninth grade. One day I expressed this idea to two of my teachers, Mrs. Sancho and Mrs. Smitty, both agreed that I should apply for the program. So, I completed the application and saw where it asked for my counselor's signature. I went to his office hoping to get his support, but I was surprised by his remarks. He looked at me as I stood outside of his door, with this look on his face that expressed he was a bit skeptical to see me after dealing with a lot of my issues early on. I proposed my attempt to apply for college credit classes at Cleveland State University and he responded suggesting that I was not prepared for that level of work. Only if you could imagine the fire that just ignited on the inside, burning with just a hint of concern that this was, yet another moment where I had been stereotyped by a professional in school.

In that moment, I felt a little disrespected and surprised to receive a discouraging statement from my counselor. Looking back at this moment, I believe he didn't mean it the way I received his statement. For all that could be true, he may have responded believing he knew what was in my best interest. Maybe, his past experience with previous students, led him to believe I may not be prepared for college level courses. But, in response to his comment, I gathered myself quickly and respectfully said, "Sir, I mean know disrespect, but you do not know me that well. I have been an "A" student my entire life. I have always been and have taken advanced classes, since I entered kindergarten. With all due respect, I will take this exam and we'll see if I'm ready." I left his office, with an unsigned application, but I was determined to return with this "I told you so" attitude. Afterwards, I felt as if there was not one person that could tell me what I can do without, first, putting effort into it. I told my two teachers what he said and they immediately called my mother on the phone and told her. Later, my mother came and had a few words with him about my academic history and we went home with a signed application ready to be submitted. I took the entry exam and when I went to pick up my results it had been expressed to me that my scores were within the 90th percentile, which was rare for high school students to score that high in both English and Mathematics. I had been advised that based on my scores, I would be ready for Calculus and English courses on the college level. I returned to Glenville High School with my results and from that moment on my counselor became a believer in my abilities.

Meanwhile, my GPA had been posted for a few weeks and the football season was over, Mrs. Smitty suggested I go meet my small school principal, Ms. Wallace. Mrs. Smitty figured that the principal needed to know who I was and by the culture of the administration, Smitty assumed she wasn't aware. It surprised me to hear that because all the previous principals that I had, knew their top and excelling students. As I walked to her office, I heard students and teachers express their curiosity about who this tenth grader was with such a GPA. I went to Ms. Wallace's office and knocked on her door. I walked in and she turned around asking who was I and asked how could she help me, I grinned and said, "Mrs. Smitty suggested I come down to introduce myself, I'm Antoinne McKinney, the student with the 4.7 GPA." This lady's face lit up so bright that I knew a difference was going to be made and that I had a purpose for being at this school now. After meeting with Ms. Wallace, I received special event invitations and exposure opportunities that led me to meet professionals and peers that became influential in my life. I could share more details about what happened from this point forward, but I'm going to end my story right here.

My academic performance at Cleveland State University allowed me to explore honors level courses at the college level. So, when I said before that the statement, "...it's not what you know, but who you know..." is a half truth, I meant that you will equally depend on both who and what you know to get you ahead. The key to this philosophy is based on how you decide to utilize the people, the knowledge, and skills together, to help you along your path to reach success.

Networking & Social Groups

During a lifetime, the relationships you develop will have some kind of impact on the person you will become and influence on the opportunities that you will receive. Your responsibility is to develop the meaning of those relationships in your life. Learning how to engage with others is a learned behavior, yet there are some basic techniques that can help you in the process. It is important to identify the relevance of your natural relationships and those that are created by your own personal interests. All relationships have a purpose, but only you can identify the significance of the connection.

Some of my natural relationships have introduced me to new people, who have also presented me with opportunities. Natural relationships are either biological associations or organically developed depending on circumstances. When you are introduced to new people, just maintain a willingness to make the connection. Then, after your initial engagement, you and the other person can determine if it would be beneficial for you both to stay connected. This form of meeting people is called networking. Networking is defined as a link of connections that develop from your associations. Networking is a skill and an opportunity. The skill of networking is learned and you develop techniques that allow you to connect with others to establish meaningful relationships for a professional advantage or personal growth. A professional advantage is when you are seeking to develop leverage for yourself in your career, place of employment, or in a competitive circumstance. Being connected to someone for a professional advantage gives you access to a different perspective and resources that may otherwise help you to achieve your goals.

It is common for people to develop personal relationships after exploring the life of another colleague. Relationships that form for personal growth are often impromptu and not intentional, but those that are intentional are often created with boundaries. For example, a parent will have a different kind of relationship with their child than the teacher that educates that same student. Both relationships are intended to support the personal growth of this child, but there are boundaries in place, so the child can distinguish between the two roles. This is the same concept when you consider to have a friend that is the same gender as your significant other or spouse.

Networking is used as a strategy to position you to reach your goals. For instance, if you are in high school and you want to be a doctor, you can easily connect with your primary care physician by having a discussion on the topic at your next checkup. If you do not have a primary care physician, there may be a clinic or some other medical facility that you can visit to attempt to connect with a doctor or other medical professionals. The purpose of going to a medical facility is not to disturb the operations, but to gather information about how you can get an opportunity to meet a medical professional about pursuing a medical career. Or, you can be a new parent that chooses to join a small group to learn about becoming an effective parent to your child(ren). Becoming a member of a social group is a unique way of networking because you are connecting with people that share a common interest. The way we can connect with people today is so far advanced compared to the past decades. In the past, networking with someone was based on the physical engagement with a person, either in a formal or an informal manner. This requires time and effort. Now we can connect with anyone in a matter of seconds by surfing social networking sites for new connections and clicking a button to connect. You have the option to send this individual a message, video, picture, or other digital items. Now, this virtual reality is redefining experiences like intimacy, engagement, sincerity, and other interactive terms. Although, society is changing with the technological advancements, the concept remains. Relationships develop and grow with meaningful engagement and your life expands once you assign a meaning to your relationships.

Support Pyramid

Natural relationships are connections that develop from biological or organic associations that are formed, usually, without your control or influence. For instance, you cannot choose your parents nor your family heritage. In time, your natural relationships will grow stronger, depending on your effort to remain connected. Relationships are a healthy part of our natural existence; and it has once been said, "It is not good that man should be alone..." (Genesis 2:18) Relationships provide support and encourage growth, so develop a support system, which is a network of people that generally care for your welfare and personal development. I have identified four relationship categories that we are bound to experience throughout life - Family, Neighborhood, Community,

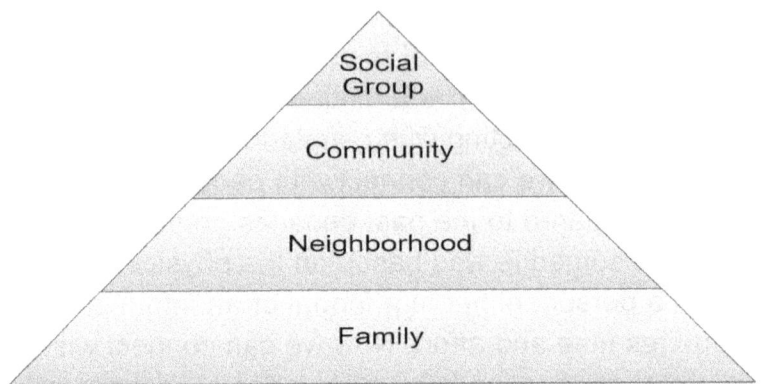

and Social Groups. I have organized these relational areas, respectively, in what I call the support pyramid; which will be used to describe the impact of these relationships on someone's life and how they can have a natural influence.

Understanding Your Connectivity

The support pyramid symbolizes the layers of encouragement that a person receives. The pyramid is divided into four layers, in order from bottom to top: 1. Family, 2. Neighborhood, 3. Community, 4. Support Groups.

The significance of each layer has three main characteristics and the dynamics of how each layer affects the motivation and perception of an individual. The first characteristic of the pyramid is the **dimension**, which indicates the theoretical portion of how much influential each type of relationship impacts an individual during their lifetime. Based on the shape of a pyramid, the sections are divided with the height evenly distributed, although the areas of each layer are proportional.

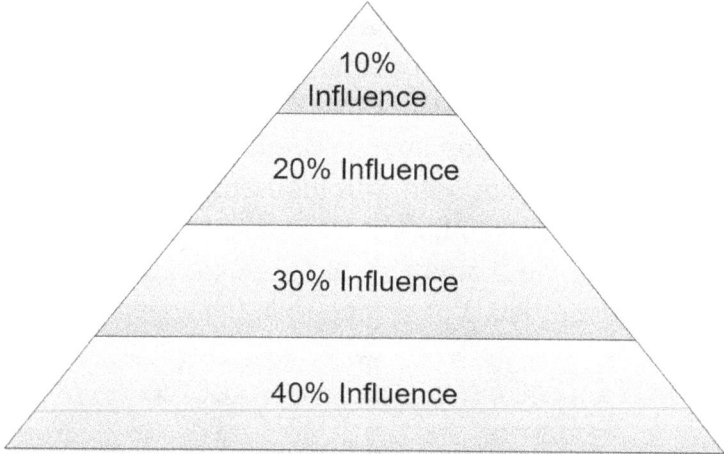

Each proportion identifies a *degree of influence* that a person or group of people can have on someone's life. See below the rationale of the percent breakdown.

1. Family - 40% of influence
2. Neighborhood - 30% of influence
3. Community - 20% of influence
4. Social Groups - 10% of influence

Given that you now have a numerical representation of how the layers may potentially influence **your** life, it is better to understand the degree of influence. The second characteristic of the pyramid is **proximity**, the closeness developed in a relationship from frequent engagement. The third characteristic of the pyramid is **position**, which can account for the role that each supporting individual has in a person's life; and is associated to the depth of their relationship.

The Layers of the Support Pyramid

Family. The 'Family' layer of the pyramid would ideally represent your relatives that have engaged with you since birth. Your immediate family would include your parents, grandparents, siblings, aunts, and uncles (your parents' siblings), and your first cousins (your aunts' and uncles' children). In this ideal situation, these relatives would be your core support as you grow up and develop in your youthful years. Unfortunately, everyone is not born with the opportunity to experience a relationship with their biological parents or relatives. For this reason, the 'Family' layer resembles people that possess the characteristics of someone in the role as a family

member. The reality for some people is that they will, more than likely, encounter someone in their lifetime that will adopt the role as a parent, grandparent, aunt, uncle, sibling or even a cousin.

We will identify this layer as the foundation of your development. The people that you would identify as family are those individuals that are present in your life to nurture your growth as well as teach and enforce basic principles to help you navigate through life. The dimension property suggests that the 'Family' layer will have the strongest influence on the decisions you will make in life. Usually, the concepts that you heed to and live out influence your thought process, which directly affects your perception and indirectly impacts your decisions. Not only, will these people influence your decisions, they will also encourage behaviors and attitudes. This leads us to the second property, proximity. The proximity suggests that ,over a period of time, you will grow physically distant from the members of this layer, without losing the *degree of influence* from those relationships. The bonds that are created in this layer, will naturally bind tighter if honesty, trust, communication, and other elements of a strong relationship are mutually exchanged. In addition, these relationships grow with frequent engagement as each person values the other. Lastly, we have the property of position that directly associates the role assigned to the individuals that fit in this category. The layer itself is positioned at the bottom because it functions like the foundation of a structure being built. The bottom layer of the pyramid is where you receive the fundamentals that are essential for living a successful and fulfilled lifestyle. If the roles of this layer are not filled by biological members, then individuals from the other three layers will organically, shift into this layer. The shift usually occurs because they become consistently supportive and the value of the relationship has been declared increasingly significant.

Neighborhood. The 'Neighborhood' layer consist of the people that you interact with frequently in your residential environment. Typically, these are the people that you encounter in common places, such as your neighborhood, school, recreation center, library, grocery store, church, and other places that you visit on a regular basis. The neighborhood group is usually the people that you share a special bond and have developed a close relationship. The difference between the family and

neighborhood layer is how you choose to engage with the people in each group on a daily basis. The people in your family circle have the benefit of interacting with you in personal and private settings. Individuals in your neighborhood space, are welcomed to interact with you in your personal space, but most of your engagement probably occurs in public places.

According to the dimension property, the people grouped in the 'Neighborhood' layer would become your secondary level of support, having about a 30% degree of influence on your life. The degree of influence for neighborhood is close to that of family because of the potential closeness that may develop over time. Typically, a friendship would start at the top of the pyramid in a lesser influential role, like an associate. As the engagements occur more often, the more acquainted you become with that individual. Hopefully, you can gain a better understanding of the relationship that is being established. Once you begin to share personal information and value the responses from people that are significant, then your relationship with them will begin to shift down the pyramid.

When a person reaches the neighborhood layer, their opinions and suggestions become significant and valuable. At this point, when your relationship gets to this layer you have accepted the person for who they are, but you have not been totally influenced by any lifestyle altering principles that they belief. Based on the proximity property, the neighborhood layer is three layers deep in the pyramid exemplifying good strength from the bond of the relationship. Bonds are created among people once trust has been established and honesty has been exchanged. The social roles that individuals have are like those that we will identify in the 'Community' layer, except for the fact that the relationship goes much deeper than the role requires. For instance, friends, coaches, co workers, mentors, teachers and so on are all roles that influence you directly, but it is optional to share personal information while you interact with them. Your awareness and perception of every person that you interact with may also influence how you may categorize their position on the pyramid.

Community. The people that you would group in the 'Community' layer are those that you encounter for a specific purpose and the relationship between you and them will not exceed beyond the standards and limitations established. For example, teachers, mentors, and coaches all have distinct reasons to be involved in your life, but are not obligated to show any interest in your personal life beyond what you may share with them. In addition, sometimes you can reveal that something personal is affecting you without verbally expressing what may be bothering you or a concern. Your behavior and attitude, which may cause interference with any relationship, can be a vital sign and give a good reason for someone to approach you about their concerns regarding your conduct. For instance, if a teacher or employer notices a change in your performance or behavior, he or she has the right to address those concerns with you. In the same respect, you have the right to share information about the real reason there may be a sudden change in your performance or behavior. Although, you may or may not feel open to share personal information, you are not obligated to do so, unless it is

an emergency or required within the means of professional relationship.

The dimension of this layer indicates a 20% degree of influence on your life. Your involvement with people in your community is important for your personal growth and development. Your relationship with these individuals are intentional and often last for a season before you no longer need to encounter them, unless you choose to establish a more personal relationship with them. The proximity of the 'Community' layer is near the top indicating that the relationship has a loose bond and can be considered a bit shallow.

Since the layer is near the top of the pyramid, this represents that you have occasional encounters, but not frequent enough to impact the relationship. The kind of people that are in this position on the pyramid may have, but not limited to, the following roles - teammates, classmates, associates, counselors, advisors, doctors, teachers, employers, and colleagues.

Social Groups. The individuals that you share common interests are classified in the 'Social Group' layer. Theoretically, your direct contact with these individuals occur more often than those in the other layers. The means of your engagement is strictly related to the interests you have in common.

The dimension of this layer is relatively small having a 10% degree of influence. The individuals that are in this category have little effect on your lifestyle habits, generally, because you only value what you share together rather than the relationship. Now, if the relationship was worth more than your common interests, then you would shift this person down to the next layer that is appropriate for the relationship. The proximity of the group means that you encounter these individuals frequently, either by choice or because of your routine. Your frequent contact with these individuals may create an opportunity for you to develop a deeper relationship. When you begin to show interest in the person, you are advocating that you have a significant interest in the person beyond your commonalities. The position or roles that people would have include, but are not limited to, clubs, small groups for a specific assembly, personal associates, and others. Unlike, the 'Community' layer, social groups do not have a purpose or reason for gathering beyond the specified interest. You could consider coworkers, classmates, or teammates as those you share interests, but your interaction is limited to specific activities related to your workplace, classroom, or team, respectively. Even then, your frequency of engagement naturally creates a bond that shifts these people down the pyramid because when bonding occurs relationships grow.

Making the Connection

Many of the relationships that I have developed were instrumental to the success I currently experience today. From birth on throughout my adulthood, I learned how to value the relationships and connections that I have developed. It wasn't until my transfer to Horizon Science Academy and the move-in with my mom's fiancée that I realized the role my family, neighborhood, friends, and teachers had in my life. When I was going through difficult times transitioning from one lifestyle to another, I depended on my relatives to help me understand how to cope with what I had a hard time grasping in this process. My father worked a lot, mainly in the 2nd and 3rd shifts, so talking with him was somewhat limited. Again, you must remember this was before cellular phones were common for communication. There was not a social media website that was age appropriate for me to use and connect with family. Neither, did I have unlimited access to my own personal computer to send instant messages. So back then, I had to depend on direct communication with my family, mainly using the home phone. As a child, there was no such thing as privacy, so I was extremely careful with what I said in front of people that I did not fully trust just yet. In addition, I was trying my best to avoid causing friction, although, I did anyway. The point is that when I needed support I immediately gravitated to the root of my support hoping to find comfort, encouragement, and advice. Then, I discovered opportunities once I started developing new relationships at Horizon Science Academy; and even when I accepted the family my mother wanted to adopt through her engagement. The moral of this story is to be aware of the people you are associated with in your life. In addition, make sure you have a good perception of their role. If you do not understand the role of a person in your circle, re-evaluate your relationship with them and reassess their position on your support pyramid .

Principle #9: Invest in Healthy Relationships

There is not one single person that is successful and can admit he or she reached success without the help or support of someone else. Even when God created the heavens and the earth, He was not alone; the Gospel of John acknowledges that,

> *"In the beginning was the Word, and the Word was with God, and the Word was God. He was in the beginning with God. All things were made through Him, and without Him nothing was made that was made." (John 1:1-3 NKJV)*

Now if He wasn't alone during the manifestation of the world, how can we assume or even think that we can become successful without the help or support from someone else. As I recall,

> *"Two are better than one, because they have a good reward for their labor. For if they fall, one will lift up his companion. But woe to him who is alone when he falls, for he has no one to help him up. Again, if two lie down together, they will keep warm; but how can one be warm alone? Though one may be overpowered by another, two can withstand him. And a threefold cord is not quickly broken. (Ecclesiastes 4:9-12 NKJV)*

Recognizing that success is not an individual experience may change how you view relationships. Relationships develop from common interests and they grow when there is a purpose. When two or more people unite for a common goal, everyone is expected to bring something to the table. Metaphorically, if you showed up to a potluck without contributing a dish, how fair would it be for you to partake in the experience and enjoy the rest of the meals? Honestly, it wouldn't be so fair. It would look like you just joined the party to take what you can get from others without having to give up anything of your own. Healthy relationships grow, when there is mutual participation, a balance of giving and receiving.

> *"As iron sharpens iron, So a man sharpens the countenance of his friend." (Proverbs 27:17 NKJV)*

As the old saying states, "birds of a feather, flock together." Elders usually advise youth to be aware of the company they wish to keep, because if they hang around someone long enough, their habits and behaviors could rub off on them. I believe it is very important that you keep people around you that model the kind of person you aspire to become and that may also have a positive influence. Let me remind you,

> *"He who walks with wise men will be wise, but the companion of fools will be destroyed." (Proverbs 13:20 NKJV)*

> *"Go from the presence of a foolish man, when you do not perceive in him the lips of knowledge." (Proverbs 14:7 NKJV)*

> *"Do not be deceived: 'Evil company corrupts good habits.'" (1 Corinthians 15:33 NKJV)*

Furthermore,

> *"Do not be unequally yoked together with unbelievers. For what fellowship has righteousness with lawlessness? And what communion has light with darkness? (2 Corinthians 6:14 NKJV)*

Conclusively, your efforts to build strong and healthy relationships depend on your ability to connect with people that can contribute to your growth. Develop a mutual commitment to one another; and support each other with encouragement and a positive influence.

Chapter Eight
Financial Stewardship

In this chapter, we will explore some very important concepts that will help you become a better steward of your most valued possessions. Oh! You thought because the title of this chapter is "Financial Stewardship" that it was all about the money? Well, you were somewhat correct. Before there were dollars and cents, there were other methods used as a medium of exchange. These mediums of exchange were often significant in their worth to society.

As I have learned through history, both biblical and world studies, I have found that items that were a rare commodity and possessions that were essential for someone's livelihood had symbolized a degree of wealth, especially if the person had excessive amounts. Therefore, this chapter on becoming a good steward of valued possessions is a conversation far beyond money. It will be a discussion about **you**; the items you own, the principles you choose to direct your life, and how you view the life you live. Why? Because these topics concern things of value, which otherwise confirms that you are valuable and are worth something.

Value What You Have

In a previous chapter, we elaborated on the importance for you to learn and understand your personal value or worthiness. Well, how do you assess the value of yourself? One way would be to identify the needs of the people around you and how well you can meet those needs with your personal assets. Even before that, think about how you value who you are, what you have, and the life that you live. Remember in chapter six, we described your personal assets as both tangible and intangible possessions. When you assign a value to those things, you are implicating what those items mean to you. Ask yourself, what makes them important and how do they improve your life. Acknowledging the value of yourself and your personal possessions, not only helps you understand your worthiness, but also creates a consciousness to care for yourself and the things you value.

When I was a kid, my cousin, Demaris, was my male role model for almost everything. I had aspired to grow up and model my lifestyle after his. Going over to visit him on the weekends was my favorite thing to do because I felt like there was a lot that I could learn from him. It seemed as if he always welcomed my presence, even among his friends. He respected my age, especially considering he was a teenager, by restricting my exposure to age appropriate things. One thing that I appreciate the most is that he demanded his peers to respect me in the same manner he did. Demaris was more like a big brother to me rather than a cousin. Whatever he did I wanted to do and wherever he went I wanted to go. I practically watched his every move and tried to mimic his behaviors and mannerisms. For instance, I saw how he collected basketball cards, Pogs, and saved money that he earned, so respectively, I became a collector of things that I valued. Demaris was the kind of young man that invested in himself, his interests, and future. He kept everything he had in good condition because he knew that it would be worth something one day. He took pride in his appearance, from his hygiene to the clothes that he wore. He had this attitude about himself as if he knew he may not be the best at certain things, but his hard work and effort would position him to become successful.

A lot of times he would put me in situations to teach me similar concepts that he believed would help me grow and become successful. The way I grew to value relationships and appreciate my possessions has derived from what I have learned from him. He showed me that I would never feel that I lacked anything, if I took care of what I already have. Caring for everything I owned, not only meant that I kept things clean and properly stored, but it also implies that I must be consciously aware of how I utilized each possession. The use of each item had to be intentional and appropriate. Even today I am very careful with all my valuables, not just the expensive items, but every item that exists within my entitlement. Most of these things are essential to the quality of life that I hope my family and I can continue to enjoy. For us to continuously enjoy these things, together, we need to be careful with how we use and handle everything we have in our possession. I am not saying accidents won't happen or mistakes will not occur, just do your best to avoid the irresponsible loss of valuable treasures.

Principle #10: Care to Give

Caring is a very important act of stewardship. It is the inspiration that allows someone to invest in the well-being of what is in their oversight. Principles like this were taught to me as a child, prior to the age of twelve, and I continued to act in such manners because I saw the benefit of doing so; believing that if I, "were faithful over few things, [I will be made] ruler over many things." (Matthew 25:21 NKJV) Hence, I still own merchandise that I have had for at least ten years or more and they are still in a fair condition. If there came a time that I no longer saw a use for an item, I would wait until I come across someone in need and would give them what I have no longer a need to keep. Stewardship also involves caring for the needs of others. I have come to understand that when we care for what we currently have, we are essentially preparing to hand it over to someone that can use it for their own need and purpose.

The act of giving is more than passing on old or used items to someone else, it is a deliberate transaction for meeting another's need, even if it means you are taking away from yourself to do so. Giving generally occurs when someone earnestly desires to enhance the livelihood and well-being of others.

"He who has a generous eye will be blessed, for he gives of his bread to the poor." (Proverbs 22:9)

"He who gives to the poor will not lack, But he who hides his eyes will have many curses." (Proverbs 28:27)

See, there is a responsibility that gives us the privilege to give back. If you are privileged, it does not always entitle you to the state of being wealthy or the membership of a dominant culture in society. A privileged person is fulfilled and blessed with all or most of their needs met. The principles of stewardship are not limited to handling finances, but extends to the privileges and possessions gained from being in your financial position.

The Double-Edge Sword

Sometimes your financial position can feel like a blessing or a curse. In the past several years, I have learned that my perception had a lot to do with how I handled my financial obligations. I can remember the one day I was down in my grandparent's basement in tears because I received a "Final Notice" from a debt collector regarding a bill I could not afford. I prayed and asked God what should I do and it hit me, "just do what is in your control, and let God handle the rest." Prior to becoming an independent adult, I received tons of advice from family and financial professionals about how to budget and manage money. When I went to college I even took a financial accounting course to learn how to handle business finances. Even with all this education, *"Anxiety"* kept creeping back into my life, knocking on the door.

"The moment Anxiety knocked on my door, I answered and let it in. Later, Anxiety gave birth to Fear, and I watched it grow over these years."

It seemed like when I started to earn just enough to keep me afloat, a drought or decrease in my income was around the corner. I mean life just continued to happen and adjustments had to be made. It was easy to blame others or even circumstances for the lack thereof, but ultimately, I learned that I only had control over how I prioritized. Once I learned, Matthew 6:32, "...For your heavenly Father knows that you need all these things." (i.e. food, hydration, clothing, and shelter) From this principle, I used my earnings to cover expenses related to these priorities first and prayed for provision over the rest.

I applied this strategy to my personal life, marriage, and business. But, Anxiety and Fear still remained in my life. It wasn't because the principle was a *false truth*, rather I just wanted results sooner than later. But, *James* once told me,

> *"My brethren, count it all joy when you fall into various trials, knowing that the testing of your faith produces patience. But let patience have its perfect work, that you may be perfect and complete, lacking nothing." (James 1:2-4 NKJV)*

Now, I have a wife, a daughter, a family, friends, and supporters that continue to BELIEVE in me, but with all the setbacks I have endured and still face, sometimes I get feelings of hopelessness and think I let them down if I have not overcome certain struggles. But, later after my birthday in September of 2016, I woke up being reminded of a quote by *Timothy*,

> *"For God has not given us a spirit of fear, but of power and of love and of a sound mind." (2 Timothy 1:7 NKJV)*

So, I testify to you today that I left Anxiety and Fear behind, by deciding to let God truly care for the things that are UNKNOWN to me in my life and I choose to walk in His perfect peace BELIEVING that He will provide and keep me and my family safe at all times. Today, I can say my debt is being cancelled, my visions are being realized, and my life is elevating to a higher level where NEW CHALLENGES await my arrival. AMEN!

Financial Responsibility

When you demonstrate your appreciation for the things you do have, you often are showing that you have a degree of responsibility to maintain them with a sense of care. In dealing with finances, in this chapter, I want you to understand that most of your tangible assets do not have a redeemable value that is relative to their original cost when you acquired them. In some instances, you may have to invest more into a product, so that you may increase its value. In addition, it will be important that you assess the monetary and personal value of each item to determine if you are acquiring more investments or expenses. Your investments are the items that you have acquired to gain other benefits, whereas, your expenses do not have additional benefits or significant return beyond their intended use. Financial stewardship refers to the way that you care for and manage your cash on hand, as well as, the responsibility for the access, purchases, and other gains acquired by your financial position, or affordability.

For all the benefits that you may receive from your financial position, you will be held accountable for the actions involving the responsibility of handling your assets. The mismanagement of or being irresponsible with your funds and assets can result in a deficit. Often when you experience this type of loss, it can have an emotional impact that could very well cause you to withdraw from social engagements, internalize your thoughts, or even second guess your future judgements. Some people develop an emotional attachment to the money and materialistic items they hold possession of, but I feel there is an in-depth reason for this connection. Our society has placed a significant need to have enough money to at least live day-to-day with the ability to afford your essentials -

rent, mortgage, utilities, transportation, food, childcare and a good portion of your debt. If either of these areas are not given proper attention, you will more than likely experience a level of hardship for a period of time. Therefore, it is important to learn how to honor, manage, and respect all your blessings and the relationships that have blessed you.

Everyone is not able to offer the same level of appreciation nor be held accountable by the same standards. You can only maintain what you have based on your own abilities, awareness, and autonomy. Every so often, people try to take on more than they can handle. As a result, they become overwhelmed with the duties and responsibilities, not allowing themselves to experience the benefits. The common goals for many people that I have encountered in my years working in social services have been to earn money, a job, a place to call their own, a car, and the ideal relationship. All of this sounds good to dream and set as a goal. Most often, these individuals are fascinated and focused on the dream that they ignore the potential outcomes or this basic principle,

> *"...For everyone to whom much is given, from him much will be required; and to whom much has been committed, of him they will ask the more." (Luke 12:48 NKJV)*

Having money is good, but if you are not aware of how to manage it, you will live like you had none to begin with. Having job experience is important, in regards to earning gainful employment, but having a job without the knowledge and skills to maintain it, reduces your chances to experience long-term employment opportunities. I'm not sure why people would rather rent a house over leasing an apartment. In my opinion, apartments offer more stability, especially for someone who is beginning to learn financial responsibility. The cost of living in an apartment seems more cost-effective than renting a house. A lot of the maintenance and expenses related to the care of your home are included in your monthly lease for an apartment. Whereas, you must incur the additional service costs by the city for waste disposal, sewer, and other fees, in addition to higher utility bills. Some landlords have limitations on your ability to perform maintenance on the rented property and you are likely to incur that expense. These are just a few of my observations as I compare the mentality of others that are driven by the appearance of their financial circumstances versus those that rationalize their decisions based on their financial position. For this reason, I believe it is better to work toward keeping what you have, rather than to work hard for what you want to get. Throughout life the more things you gain, the more responsibility you may incur; and with responsibility comes accountability.

Steps for Financial Management

When you are handling actual cash, whether it is through a bank account or in a safe, it can entice you to spend your money at your leisure. As easy as it may seem, there are various things to consider before you can swipe a card or hand over your money to the cashier. You have financial obligations that need your attention. Before you reach this moment, you need to stop and think about how you can best utilize your funds to get the most out of your financial decisions. This sounds so elementary, but I assure you that one time or another you thought buying fast food or takeout was not going to harm anything, just this one time. For that one time, you may have been right; but what about the consecutive times after that one? Learning efficient and effective ways to manage your money will help you make better decisions and improve your financial position. Financial management includes the planning, allocation, organizing, monitoring, and controlling of your finances. Heed these steps of financial management and you will have an improved experience making worthy financial decisions.

Step 1: Plan

1.1 Identify Income Opportunities. Although it may seem like a natural occurrence or common sense, I must emphasize the importance of learning how to maximize your income potential. The essence of meeting someone's need, either in-person or through a business, creates your income potential. Before you determine what need you can meet for someone, assess yourself for skills and tasks that you can perform well, also include those that you have not yet mastered. Of course, the skillsets you are most familiar with would be those that you capitalize from first. Then, continue to improve upon the skills that need more attention and practice. Performing chores to get an allowance is a good way to practice the employer and employee relationship. But, maybe for some teenagers and young adults, landscaping or other labor related work may be more appropriate. Either way, you should figure out the needs that are around you, your capacity to meet those needs, and decide how you will enter the market.

1.2 Develop Savings Plan. However, you decide to make a legitimate income, consider your options to save a portion of the money you make to establish financial stability, as well as, secure funds in case of an emergency. For individuals that have high debt-to-income ratios 80% or more, I would recommend to start by saving less than 10% of your monthly income. This way you can address your financial obligations with the majority of your income. If your debt-to-income ratio is less than 50%, I would consider that you still save a portion of your income for an emergency savings, but also consider ways that you could use a fraction of your excess income for investment opportunities that fit your circumstances. Be sure to consult a financial planner or other financial professional to guide you in the right direction.

1.3 Create Spending Restrictions. Placing restrictions on your spending requires discipline and consistency to develop good practices and self-control. In addition to these parameters, identify your spending priorities, such that you can remain faithful to your financial commitments. For example, a person may prioritize their finances in this manner: (1) Tithes and Offerings (2) Primary Living Expenses (i.e. includes rent, mortgage, and utilities) (3) Food or Groceries (4) Debt Cancellation (5) Leisure. Further restrictions may include limitations on your spending activities, allowances for spending categories, identifying due dates, schedule payments, and methods for how you access funds.

1.4 Setup Accountability Measures (Financial Management Applications). One of the most challenging aspects of managing money is keeping yourself accountable for your decisions and your plan. It is always good to have someone else that is neutral to your financial obligations to become identified as your accountability partner. Some accountability partners are financial professionals, parents, entrusted friends, or financial institutions. Your accountability partner will be responsible for making sure you stay on course with your financial plan. The two of you will organize meetings, audits, and other functions necessary to make sure you are acting within the means of your plan. In addition to having an accountability partner, you may want to consider the use of financial applications that can serve as a database for your financial information and other management functions. There are software applications that are compatible with mobile devices, computers, and cloud-base interfaces. Use these applications as an accountability tool and a way for you to evaluate your commitment to the financial plan you have created or that has been created for you by a professional.

Step Two: Allocate

Once you have generated your thoughts, organized your ideas, and gathered all the pieces for your financial strategy, you are now ready to execute your plan. In this step of financial management, you will need to write down or create some documentation that will list your current and actual net income. Your net income will be the amount that you receive on your paycheck, so that you can begin the allocation process using available funds, rather than your gross income to deduct your expenses.

2.1 Itemize Expenses. List all your recurring expense items, their frequency, and dollar amounts. Once you have all the expenses listed subtract your total expenses from your net monthly income (net income - total expenses). In some instances, you may have semi-annual or quarterly expenses; if you encounter this situation allocate the appropriate portions to account for the monthly value in your monthly expenses. This list creates more awareness of the transactions that will occur each month. You will be surprised how often people, who seem to have everything together, are not quite this attentive to their finances like they should. Next, consider your monthly or frequent activities that will result in a financial transaction. For instance, grocery shopping, child care, healthcare appointments, property maintenance, pet care, and other expenses with variable costs. Some of these frequent activities are not recurring at the same time which also impacts the consistency of your spending.

2.2 Create a Budget. When you think of a budget you probably get nervous because you will need to become more conscious of the things you purchase or even want to buy. Some people shy away from creating a budget because of their bad relationship with Math. Others may shy away from the meticulous involvement that may be required to create their budget and either the maintenance, thereafter. You also have individuals that do not want to be aware of the reality regarding their expenses for a variety of reasons, one being that anxiety builds up from fear of not having enough financial security to pay for their expenses.

However, there are people willing to face this challenge and desire to learn good strategies to create a budget that works for them. Let me get you in on a little secret, if you made your itemized list, you basically have created a draft of your budget. At this point, the only thing you need to concern is how you want to format and design the budget document. In addition, determine if you want to use a software application or a sheet of paper to duplicate your budget and later use as a reference. I would recommend that you create the reference copy of your budget with Microsoft Excel or a similar spreadsheet application, which will allow you to customize formulas to calculate specific information. Using other applications that record your accounting information, may allow you to create a budget using their templates and formats as well. If you have not written your itemized list of expenses, do so to maintain an accurate calculation on the budget to project your TRUE financial position.

2.3 Plan Spending Activities. Your personal financial position is determined by understanding your debt-to-income ratio as it may allow or deny the opportunity to gain access to financial resources, purchase high-priced items, and other financial benefits. If you have a significantly high debt-to-income ratio, your freedom to spend the money you earned will be slim to none; you may in fact live paycheck to paycheck. If you can use a calendar to mark your expenses on their due date, you can analyze your cash flow to determine if you have a specific window of opportunity to spend a portion of your excess cash for priority spending. Priority spending is being able to purchase significant items that may not be on your recurring budget, but within a reasonable timeframe, you can purchase them knowing when you will have enough funds available. One of the benefits of priority spending is that you can plan for future purchases and take the time to thoroughly research the products you need.

Step Three: Monitor

Money is a tool, nonetheless a resource, for people to use and experience a certain quality of life. Although money is typically used for purchasing goods and services, there are ways that people can misuse funds and illegally obtained significant amounts. By no means, am I suggesting that you may have any thoughts to do so, but it is important for you to understand the concept of financial monitoring to avoid mistakes, bad habits, and be aware of any potential illegal transactions. There are concerns of identity theft, laundering, unauthorized transactions, fraud and much more that any person is subject to encounter. You may be an innocent bystander, but learning more about these activities and how you can develop practices to prevent them is the best way to protect your assets and identify from these activities. The best actions of financial monitoring for individuals are to (1) keep records of your transactions by using a ledger or saving bank statements; (2) limit the access of your financial information to other people; (3) secure your funds with a financial institution or a personal safe; (4) periodically review the records of recent transactions, in other words, reconcile your records frequently. By actively taking these measures to monitor your finances you can safeguard your assets and reduce exposure to illegal activities.

Step Four: Control

Control your finances. Make sure that after you have applied your financial plan and execute your strategies, verify your actual expenditures with your budgeted expenses. Perform monthly, quarterly, or annual audits to make sure your values match your itemized categories. Comparing your budget items to your actual purchases will help to understand any patterns, changes to your spending habits, and identify potential areas that can create a savings. Controlling your finances is another way of saying be actively aware of where your money comes from, where it is going, and how you can maintain or improve your financial position.

Being a good steward overall helps you to become a better person and overseer of responsibility. Money is just a resource to help you navigate through life. Do not let money become the focus of why you work or do anything in life. Let your work ethics become a representation of your character. Any financial or material gain should be treated like a bonus check for doing more than the average person around you. Let the inspiration that lies within you, keep you encouraged and motivated.

Message to the Reader

Dear Reader,

Thank you for taking the time to read my first authorship. Originally, I began to write this book as a narrative to my success management and planning curriculum, but I realized that my experiences have become an influence to what I have just shared with you.

I understand that people recognize success differently, but the concept of it will always be the same. It doesn't matter if you are a youth, adult, senior, a professional, parent, entrepreneur, a member of the Church, or any other person in this world, you all are aiming to achieve goals and aspire to live dreams that you can only imagine.

These concepts and principles may have proven their relevance in your life, but do not attempt to act out behaviors in their resemblance. Rather, rightfully execute each principle because you believe in their benefits. Once you have activated these principles, you are committing yourself to a lifestyle that rewards you with a sensation of success beyond a materialistic point of view.

So, stay encouraged, be inspired, and live motivated to conquer all that you can obtain for the enjoyment of your life and the experiences within it.

Sincerely,

Antoinne M. McKinney

Message to the Reader

A SPECIAL DEDICATION

The Inspiration That Lies Within...

This book is the beginning of a series that I have decided to dedicate to my family. Although, I have specific individuals that I will acknowledge later, the bulk of my inspiration behind this book is due to the love and support my family has given me for the past 25+ years. Being the first grandchild on both sides of my family, presented itself with great rewards, but the expectations were also great by their demands. Being that I was born an African-American boy in a time when opportunities were available, my grandparents and my parents pushed me to do my best regardless of the odds that were against me. In addition, I added another standard that I hope to pass down to my children, which is that I wanted to make sure I resembled, at the very least, the positive aspects of my parents, while aiming to go beyond their achievements.

I believe a legacy is left, not only to leave something behind for the next generation, but also to challenge them to higher standards. A legacy can also bring awareness to the successor about their roots and their effort potential. Effort potential is the minimum capacity for a person to maintain the willingness to do something, but they have not executed or released this potential. There were moments in my live when I declared I wanted to aim for excellence in all that I do. Although, I was young and not able to do much except excel in school and recreational sports, I continued to nurture this desire until I had been able to exert the potential that stayed dormant.

In these moments, I acknowledged that I wanted to make sure the people, I care about and that cared about me would have something to always remember me by. Like I mentioned in my preface, my great-great grandmother whispered, "Make Me Proud," in my ear when I was just a small boy. I am not sure exactly the time frame of when she passed away after that moment but, I would always recall her saying that to me anytime I had faced adversity.

In addition, my parents are another reason why I value my experiences and have become inspired to excel in life. My parents were just about to enter their 20's when they had me. During that time, I am sure the culture of society had different stigmas on young adults, who were unmarried with a child. Because of this fact and other factors regarding my parents' choosing to accept me, I made a commitment to live my life in honor of them for giving me a chance to be their son and achieve beyond what they have accomplished.

Furthermore, I have to give credit where credit is due. I was born, blessed with four grandmothers, two grandfathers, a ton of aunts & uncles, and older cousins that all took part in watching over me. As the saying goes, "...it takes a village to raise a child;" and believe me I know this to be true. Just about everyone that I know in my family, spent some quality time imparting some wisdom or life lessons, so that I may avoid some of their mistakes. I hope this book resembled some of the knowledge and wisdom I received.

Lastly, my inspiration to excel grew deeper once I learned that I had to lead by example for my younger brother and cousins that I grew up with for a fraction of my youth. Knowing that there were a younger set of eyes always watching me, I grew a subconscious about every single thing that I chose to do, especially in public. It wasn't that I just wanted to model good behavior, I wanted to create a path for them to avoid unnecessary struggles. I hope that the success I have achieved, created a path that will continue to inspire and encourage them to persevere and remain persistent with their goals and aspirations in life.

Unfortunately, during the production of this book I lost two people that were very inspirational to me as I kept myself steady on this journey. I will mention one in this section and the other will be in the Acknowledgements.

In the loving memory of Aaron N. Blake (1997-2016), who was born as a twin and the first to be born. He obtained a lot of recognition from his affiliations. His twin and himself, both, graduated from high school in 2015, then advanced to attend Lakeland Community College. During high school and college, he competed against others in basketball, which he was most passionate toward. While in college, he had been employed to become a professional landscaper. But, on the eve of Thanksgiving in 2016, he gained his salvation to be with his Heavenly Father for eternity.

This publication shall also honor the family members that I have lost. Within the past 15 years, between 2001 and 2016, at least, three of my cousins lost their lives as they were trying to find their position in this world. All of them were under the age of 30, but the most recent loss was the youngest at the age of 19. This book shall honor all of them by becoming a guide to teenagers and young adults, who may need that extra guidance to find their way in life with the right kind of support. This is very important because like I stated earlier in the book, "We all have a lifetime to manage, but there is no guarantee for how long we shall live to manage it." This statement is meant to express the sense of urgency to live out your purpose. I will continue to miss their physical presence, but I could never forget their role and influence on my life; so as long as I live, I will strive to become an inspiration to others as they were to me.

Acknowledgments

One thing that I have learned and valued in my lifetime is thanksgiving. No, I am not talking about the annual "food" holiday. (For those that know me that was kind of an inside joke.) But, I am referring to the general idea of giving thanks, in other words, acknowledging your appreciation or thankfulness toward others for what they have done for you. There are several people that I would like to recognize individually for what they have done in my life and the support they have given in the process of creating this book.

God. First and foremost, I give honor and the glory to God for this opportunity to share this portion of my life as an inspiration to all that have been able to read it. This book explicitly shares how Godly principles have guided my life to fulfill a purpose. Meanwhile, these principles stirred up a fire of inspiration that kept me steadfast, especially in the midst of trials, setbacks, and other moments of vulnerability. So, if this book has had any impact on your life, please know that I will only take credit for sharing my story, with the hope it would encourage others and you to choose a healthier lifestyle that is led by good principles and strong beliefs.

My Pastors. I would like to thank all of my pastors for helping me to learn how to study the Word of God, comprehend revelations, and interpret the written language to translate into modern concepts. In addition, I am thankful that they all encouraged the need to balance an individual relationship with God and corporate fellowship with assembled Believers, while not forsaking others who have not committed to a Godly lifestyle. I have learned that Love and Compassion from a Believer to a non-Believer speaks volumes because then we allow the Spirit of God to manifest itself outwardly to the people around us.

Frank Feola, PhD. Dr. Feola was my academic advisor during my two years at Cleveland State University in the Post-secondary Enrollment Options Program. Dr. Feola was someone that I would talk to when I need some inspiration throughout my experience at Cleveland State University. He was very understanding and he knew that I had a desire to seek challenges. One day during a time when we were planning my schedule for an upcoming semester, he asked how would I feel about taking an honors class? At this point, I was confused because I barely held onto a 3.0 GPA this semester and secondly, how could a high school student enroll into a college honors class? In my opinion, that's not even the oddest part of the story. Not only was he trying to enlist me for an honors class, which I learned later was so he could offer me an honors level scholarship to CSU, but also he enlisted me into an Honors Physics class, which was a bit accelerated. At first, I agreed because it sounded good and I needed that class to graduate; but the experience was intense and challenging, especially the evening commutes on the bus trying to get to my labs. (Inside Joke: If you are a Clevelander, you understand that RiTA is just as reliable as the weather.)

Overall, I am glad that he challenged me to take this higher level course because I discovered college honors was the level where I was challenged most and still performed quite well among my classmates. Years later, I invited Dr. Feola to join the board of directors for a non-profit that I established back when I was in high school. He accepted the invitation and aided me during the process of creating the Success Management and Planning curriculum. He participated in the pilot initiatives that tested my theories and concepts. He kept me accountable to my goals and encouraged me with affirmation that I needed to write this book. Although, he is no longer with us to see the manifestation of his influence on my life, not only do I acknowledge his support in this process, but I also dedicate this authorship to be part of his legacy as a father, husband, son, and any other role that allowed him to connect with people and aspire them to look at life through a different pair of lens..

Rhonda Crowder. Rhonda, with her professional expertise and experience as an associate publisher has been willing to guide me through the process of publishing this authorship, as my FIRST book! I am so thankful to have her support, not only because of her professional contribution, but also for her friendship. If you recall the Support Pyramid, Rhonda was one of those individuals that gradually moved from a person that I met at a community event, when Bill Cosby came to Cleveland. She also was the journalist that captured my remarks at the forum and later interviewed me about what I had expressed. Since then, she has continued to support me through my endeavors and professional growth. For this reason, I truly appreciate her willingness to aide me through the editing, review, and production process.

Andrew "Kid Retro" Bailey. Andrew, is an aspiring graphics design and is a cousin that has always been like another brother. Andrew and I grew up very close when we were kids, so to have someone help me graphically articulate my the concept design for the book cover. He really was great to work with and he gave a lot of attention to the idea that I saw with my imagination, but he brought it to real life. His draft truly inspired the final version.

There are other individuals that have had an indirect influence on my life that inspired some of the content that I shared. These individuals are anonymous, but I just want to acknowledge that I appreciate their encouragement and eagerness to push me beyond my limits so that I can continue to be an inspiration to others.

About the Author

Antoinne M. McKinney is a young professional with experience that has given him valuable exposure to different industries and several career disciplines. Antoinne holds a Bachelor of Arts degree in Urban Studies from Cleveland State University. He has participated in the 14-week Java coding bootcamp at Tech Elevator, where he learned how to develop dynamic web based software systems using the Java programming language and platform.

Currently, he serves as a staff member for the FirstGen Center at Notre Dame College (South Euclid, Ohio), where he supports the establishment of a new department that provides focused support and mentoring for students who are considered the first in their family to graduate from college .

At the age of 15, Antoinne embarked on his entrepreneurial journey to establish the nonprofit, Young A.D.U.L.T.S. Inc. This organization has become a vehicle to support and inspire youth and families with strategies to overcome socio-economic challenges, as they pursue a healthier lifestyle. In addition, he and his wife provide digital media services through their business, Simcha Media.

Beyond his professional endeavors, Antoinne enjoys spending time with his family and keeping up with a few hobbies, which include traveling, fishing, writing, and exploring his interest with computers and technology. He passionately embraces the opportunity to uplift his community with inspiration. He aspires to become a leader of change and innovation in urban communities, so that one day he may inspire the next generation of leaders and working class citizens.

About the Author

A dear friend once said, *"Antoinne M. McKinney doesn't "think small" or "think in the now". On the contrary, he sees things through a global lens and projects into the future a vision of what could be if a solid foundation can be set now. Mr. McKinney is a visionary and tops that off with a true heart of love and compassion for all. He believes that all people should have access to personal and professional excellence no matter the race, culture or socioeconomic status. In raising the level of performance and instilling a desire for excellence in individuals, he believes that the social landscape can benefit; creating a more compassionate and caring society."*

For more information about <u>Antoinne</u>, visit www.antoinnemmckinney.com.

For more information about <u>Simcha Media</u>, visit www.simcha-media.com.

For more information about <u>Young A.D.U.L.T.S. Inc.</u>, visit www.youngadultsinc.com.

Bonus Chapter
What's Next...

After my wife read the first draft of this book, she was very excited about the material and the information that she had reviewed. The only problem for her was that she expected to read more about what she could do next. She was ready to put forth the effort to execute the principles stated and adopt the concepts described, but she did not know how. So, this is why I am writing to you the next steps to help you apply these principles and concepts to your life.

But first, it is important to grasp and gain some understanding about your destiny. Your destiny will spark motivation and give you some direction to narrow down the route you should take to achieve your goals. Perhaps, you do not have an idea about what you desire or how you would like to live in the future. I highly suggest that you get out of your comfort zone and expose yourself to new things that can have a positive affect on your life. This will help you to discover what you like and do not like. When you identify the things you do not like, investigate what turned you away from having any interest. I can go on and on about discovering yourself, but that would take away from the adventure. Therefore, before going to step one of the next steps, take ample time to discover who you are, what you like, how you wish to live, where you would like to go, who you would like to meet, etc. Once you have discovered more information about yourself, you will be ready to take the **NEXT STEPS**!

1. **Write Down Your Dreams**

The first thing that you should do is write down all your dreams and aspirations. Some people would prefer to create a vision board, but the vision board does not capture **your** personal preferences and desires. You may identify the concepts or material items that you would like, but you cannot capture your feelings, nor how you may see yourself waking up everyday living the better portion of your life. This is why, I am suggesting that you **WRITE IT DOWN!**

When you start to ponder on your dreams do not let your RE-ALITY short change your thoughts by **only** thinking about what you believe is possible. Allow yourself to THINK BIG, beyond what you can fathom, and become aware of your unexplored passions. Your passions can be seen as a driving force that ultimately keep you inspired when you are dealing with challenging moments. With this step, you should tap into your inspiration and ignite a flame that will continue to burn, only if you choose to fuel your desire to pursue your dreams.

2. Develop Your Strategic Approach

Your strategic approach is an action plan that considers what you are able to do, your willingness to commit to a course of action, and your precision when applying your best effort to achieve goals. Your capacity is based on the limitations of both your strengths and weaknesses. Although, you may be strong in some areas and need improvement in others, you still have limitations that restrict your abilities. These restrictions are not barriers, they are opportunities for growth.

Without your willingness to remain committed to your plan, you will lack the endurance required to withstand the challenges and storms that will arise in the process. On your pursuit to happiness, it will not be all sunshine and rainbows, but rather partly cloudy mixed with rain and some thunderstorms. I'm telling you that the atmosphere of your journey to reach success is like broadcasting the weather as if you live in the Midwestern region of the United States. You will hardly know what the true weather conditions will be until the day comes, **JUST BE READY!**

Be consistent. Be concise. Be real. If you are serious about pursuing your dreams, you cannot afford to pretend to be someone or something that you are not. It is okay to make adjustments or even grow into new habits, but do not think that because you are highly motivated now that you will just make a huge shift into a new lifestyle. It is important that you choose to live a lifestyle with a routine of small successes. This way you can develop instinctive habits that yield positive results. In other words, if you are successful at achieving minor objectives, you will learn how to accomplish major goals.

When you are ready to develop your strategic plan, refer back to *Chapter 2: Plan Your Goal the S.M.A.R.T. Way*. Then, use the *S.M.A.R.T. Goal Planning* worksheet in the back of the book to help you think about the key factors needed to turn your dreams into reality. When you get to the "Rely" section of the process, this is where you begin to analyze your reason for pursuing your goal, as well as, discover whether you need to achieve something else before pursuing this goal. This is a good way to assess your goal priorities.

The *S.M.A.R.T. Goal Planning* worksheet can be used to create an outline of information that describes the details of your action plan. Once you have developed your strategic approach ask someone that you feel is trustworthy to become your accountability partner. An accountability partner is a support that will make sure you remain committed to your plan and other responsibilities.

3. Assess How You rePresent Yourself

In case you were wondering, I intentionally spelled "rePresent" this way because this step is going to talk about how you present yourself repeatedly in different areas. Before we begin, you may want to refresh your mind by reading *Chapter 4: Social & Professional Imagery*.

After reviewing the content and the concepts described, you should remember that we briefly covered the importance of making sure your image is fairly consistent as you engage with others in different environments. In the chapter, I described how each individual has three personas - *personal*, *professional*, and *public*. What I did not specify is that you will usually present these images in four environments (i.e. *academic, social, domestic,* and *professional*) as you go about your day. The more consistent you are with your behaviors, attitude, and conduct, people can learn the kind of person you are and you can experience more growth.

The manner, in which, you rePresent yourself in multiple environments has a lasting impact on your engagement, relationships, and opportunities. Each environment has a different atmosphere, but with a few adjustments you should, comfortably, maintain your character. You will not only represent yourself well, but also you will attract positivity.

You can measure or assess how you rePresent yourself by using the *Success Management & Planning Self-Assessment* that can be found in the back of the book. This assessment measures your position for developing a successful lifestyle. Once you have your results, you will be able to identify areas that need improvement.

What Does This Mean For My Role?

When you are thinking about these next steps, your outcomes will differ if you begin to think about your individual roles. Thinking of the next steps from an individual perspective will help you identify your personal interests, wants and desires. Approaching these next steps from a role perspective, will help you define your purpose, not only in that role but also in life. Therefore, I would suggest that you make a list of the additional roles you have in life; use the support pyramid to help you identify who you are to other people. After you make this list, go back through these steps to discover what you desire for yourself in each role. Now, the rest is up to you, so live a healthy lifestyle for the right reasons.

SMART Goal Planning

SMART Goal Planning

This SMART Goal Planning process will help you to simplify the details about any goal you hope to achieve that is relevant to your education, career exploration, employment search, or finances.

The following questions are to help you outline the details of a strategic plan regarding how you will approach your goal.

Name:_____

Select the type of goal you will be setting.

1. *Educational - a goal that focuses on the growth of your learning ability*

2. *Career Exploration - a goal that explores your interest in a particular field or subject that will define or express the potential for a long-term work experience (i.e. college planning, volunteer work, internship, etc.)*

3. *Job Placement/Employment - a goal to find and secure an opportunity for the purpose of gaining income or to build upon compensated work experience*

4. *Financial - a goal to manage, increase, save, or invest monetary resources to support basic living needs and educational expenses*

Specify...

In this section, you will describe your goal, identify the potential benefits, state your anticipated sacrifices, and share the opportunities that may come from achieving this goal.

SMART Goal Planning

1. In one sentence, state your goal.

2. Once you have achieved this goal, what would be the benefits? List them. (i.e. What are the expected positive outcome?)

3. What sacrifices will you have to make to accomplish this goal? (i.e. Who or what will affect your commitment to achieve this goal?)

4. Describe any future opportunities that this goal will help to prepare you for or put you in the position to pursue later.

Measure...

In this section, you will list your objectives; brainstorm what can signify any type of progress; and create a timeline for when you expect to complete each task.

1. List the specific tasks that will guide you toward reaching your goal.

2. Brainstorm other signs that may measure the progression toward your goal.

3. Identify dates that seem reasonable for you to complete your above listed tasks or objectives.

Access...

In this section, you will identify assets (i.e. resources, skills, devices, tools, and resourceful individuals) that will become useful to help you throughout the execution of your strategic plan. In addition, you will need to list individuals that can hold you accountable to your plan and back-up strategies.

1. *Think for a moment.* What assets do you have that can help you to achieve your tasks and objectives?

List the items, skills, people, organizations, groups, other types of assets that seem suitable.

2. Who do you know that can hold you accountable to stay focused on this goal based on the plan you are creating? List the names of the people and their relationship to you.

Rely...

In this section, you will identify any dependencies related to this goal. There are two types of dependents: 1) people or something to be dependent upon you achieving this goal or 2) things that must be accomplished prior to you starting to pursue this goal.

1. What people or things are dependent upon you achieving this goal? How would they be affected by this goal?

2. Is there anything that needs to be accomplished prior to pursuing this goal? If so, this would be the goal to pursue first.

Time Frame...

In this section, you will set the time frame that you anticipate to have this goal achieved. Upon achieving your goal please note the date accomplished and update your status.

1. When do you plan to start working toward your goal?

2. When do you expect to have, your goal achieved?

3. When did you start your goal?

4. When did you achieve your goal?

Success Management & Planning
SELF-ASSESSMENT

The Inspiration That Lies Within...

Success Management & Planning Self-Assessment

Please complete the following assessment questions. Your honesty is crucial to receive accurate results. The survey should take approximately ten minutes or less to complete.

In addition to your assessment, you may ask an educator, family member, friend, associate or professional to complete this assessment to provide you with insight about yourself. Make sure that other people are ONLY assessing the environments that they engage with you.

Name: _____

Date of Assessment: _____

Type of Assessment

- Pre-Assessment (1st assessment)
- Post-Assessment (take at least two weeks after the 1st assessment)

Mark the option that best describes your relationship to the participant.

- I am the Participant
- Educator or School Administrator
- Friend/Associate/Mentor
- Family Member/Relative
- Coach/Supervisor/Other Professional Associate

Academic Environment

Rating Scale: 0=Not Applicable; 1=Less Likely; 2=Sometimes; 3=Often; 4=Likely; 5=Very Likely

SMP Self-Assessment

Educators or school administrators, please rate the participant's ability to do the following:

1. respect peers
2. complete class assignments
3. complete homework assignments
4. participate in class lectures
5. participate in class activities
6. respect teachers at school
7. respect administrators at school
8. receive help or support outside of the classroom

Social Environment

Rating Scale: 0=Not Applicable; 1=Less Likely; 2=Sometimes; 3=Often; 4=Likely; 5=Very Likely

Friend, associate, or mentor, please rate the participant's ability to do the following:

1. associate with positive individuals
2. engage in positive activities
3. help or support others
4. seek help or support from others
5. communicate clearly
6. communicate respectfully

Domestic Environment

Rating Scale: 0=Not Applicable; 1=Less Likely; 2=Sometimes; 3=Often; 4=Likely; 5=Very Likely

Family member, guardian, or relative, please rate the participant's ability to do the following:

1. take on household responsibility
2. respect others in the household
3. participate in family activities
4. initiate or come up with family activities
5. obey household rules
6. obey parental authority
7. be at peace in your home

Professional Environment

Rating Scale: 0=Not Applicable; 1=Less Likely; 2=Sometimes; 3=Often; 4=Likely; 5=Very Likely

Coach, supervisor, or other professional, please rate the participant's ability to do the following:

1. pay attention during training exercises
2. actively participate in training exercises
3. communicate respectfully to others
4. complete tasks independently
5. complete tasks with a team or group
6. complete projects independently
7. complete projects with a team or group
8. comply with rules
9. arrive on time

www.ingramcontent.com/pod-product-compliance
Lightning Source LLC
Chambersburg PA
CBHW070947180426
43194CB00041B/1709